ABBA! FATHER!

Meditations on Jesus' Prayers on the Way to the Cross

Vernon R. Schreiber

AUGSBURG Publishing House • Minneapolis

ABBA! FATHER!
Meditations on Jesus' Prayers on the Way to the Cross

Scripture quotations unless otherwise noted are from the Revised Standard Version of the Bible, copyright 1946, 1952, and 1971 by the Division of Christian Education of the National Council of Churches.

Scripture quotations marked TEV are from The Good News Bible, Today's English Version, copyright 1966, 1971, 1976 by American Bible Society. Used by permission.

Scripture quotations marked NEB are from The New English Bible. Copyright The Delegates of the Oxford University Press and The Syndics of the Cambridge University Press, 1961, 1970. Reprinted by permission.

Some material on pp. 46-47 is from *A Man for All Seasons,* by Robert Bolt. Copyright © 1960, 1962 by Robert Bolt. Reprinted by permission of Random House Inc.

ISBN 0-8066-2389-6   LCCN 88-83594

Manufactured in the U.S.A.   APH 10-0121

1   2   3   4   5   6   7   8   9   0   1   2   3   4   5   6   7   8   9

*To my wife Jane and
to all those companions through the years whose prayers,
for me and with me,
have brought to me the strong presence of the Lord.*

CONTENTS

Preface   7

1. How Jesus Began His Task   9
   John 18:1, Luke 22:39

2. Jesus' Prayer for Our Spiritual Healing   15
   Luke 22:31,32

3. Jesus' Prayer of Surrender   22
   Mark 14:32-36

4. The Ultimate Goal of Jesus' Prayers   29
   John 12:27,28

5. Jesus' Prayer of Forgiveness   35
   Luke 23:34

6. Jesus' Prayer into the Silence of God   43
   Matthew 27:46

7. Jesus' Prayer for Our Oneness   50
   John 17:20-21

8. Jesus Shows Us How to Die   56
   Luke 23:46

9. He Lives to Plead for Me Above   63
   John 20:11-18

10. What We Have Learned   70

Shouts, Cries, and Prayers: Psalms for the   74
   Days of Lent

PREFACE

How do the prayers of Jesus on the way to the cross help us pray in the most critical periods of life? His prayers show us how every task should be begun. They show us Christ as the healer of his wounded followers. They show us how to surrender to God, and point us to the chief end of all prayer life. They help us pray for the forgiveness of others, and teach us to face death. They lead us into a spirit of oneness with others and with God. They remind us that Jesus Christ lives today and still prays for us.

The apostle Paul once exhorted his young co-worker Timothy to preach the word "in season and out of season." Because this book examines Jesus' prayers during the last days and hours of his life, it can provide ideas for reflection during the season of Lent. Because these prayers deal with those critical moments which are a part of our lives throughout the year, it is also a book for every season.

If the central themes are used on a weekly basis, the psalms listed in this book's final section can be used in daily prayer as a means of reinforcing the theme for that week. The reader is invited to reproduce the meditations based on those psalms for distribution to other worshipers or prayer partners.

However this book might be used, it approaches the subject of prayer with an awareness that prayer is always more than a set of words. It is the expression of a living relationship with God. This fundamental aspect of prayer is suggested in the book's title: *Abba! Father!* These words first came from the lips of Jesus himself when he prayed to God using this term of endearment. In so doing, he introduced to the people of God a new dimension in prayer, encouraging a spirit of confidence and trust.

It would be a great mistake, however, to imagine that Jesus was free from the struggles that are a part of our efforts at prayer. We tend to pass over too quickly the picture of Jesus at prayer as it is given to us in the letter to the Hebrews: "In the days of his flesh, Jesus offered up prayers and supplications, with loud cries and tears, to him who was able to save him from death, and he was heard for his godly fear" (Heb. 5:7).

"With loud cries and tears. . . ." This phrase calls to mind the nature of many of the great prayers in the book of Psalms. It succinctly describes how Jesus prayed as he drew near to the cross. At every step of the way he turned to the Father. In every prayer, while his words ascended in shouts, cries, and whispers, he revealed his sense of sonship as he asked for the strength to carry out the mission given to him. Whether he was facing a hostile crowd, his frightened disciples, the loneliness of Gethsemane, or the agony of the cross, it was always as our brother in the flesh that he called God as his Father.

It was these prayers to his "Abba, Father" that kept Jesus on course as he marched to the cross. If we are to take up our cross and follow after him, then we must learn from him how to pray. May God through his Spirit grant that these meditations on Jesus' prayers on the way to the cross will enable all who would follow him to prevail in their own struggles. May they share not only in their Lord's sufferings, but in his Easter triumph as well.

1
HOW JESUS BEGAN HIS TASK

When Jesus had spoken these words, he went forth with his disciples across the Kidron valley, where there was a garden, and he and his disciples entered.

John 18:1

And he came out, and went, as was his custom, to the Mount of Olives; and the disciples followed him.

Luke 22:39

What tasks are facing you this moment? Perhaps you are thinking of a difficult assignment given to you. Or the making of a hard decision. Or picking up the pieces after a broken romance or a shattered marriage. Or dealing with serious illness. Even when we face no great crisis, the very nature of our passing from one age group to the next, or from one set of responsibilities to another, places us in a situation of making a new beginning. Our answers may vary in their details, but in all likelihood every one of us would admit that we wish our prayers played a greater role in finding the answers we need.

Our lost handle on prayer

Part of our difficulty lies in the fact that we do not live in a praying world. It is a frightened and frantic world, but it is not a world that knows how to pray. It would like to pray, but it has given up on prayer. It is a world that contains many people who prayed once, but pray no more. They are gifted, and they do their best to meet the challenges of a troubled world and to become worthwhile persons themselves. But through it all they feel isolated from the presence of God and alone in their struggle. They have lost the handle on prayer.

It should not surprise us that in a world of unbelief, even those who say that they believe in the existence of God find it difficult to pray. In fact, they find it difficult even to let it be known that they pray. The traditional Ash Wednesday Gospel lesson contains Jesus' warning against going out into the streets to pray to be noticed. That's one fault we don't have to worry about! If we're in a restaurant, we pray as furtively as two junior choir members passing a note in the choir loft. We try to finish before the waiter comes and catches us. I recall one person telling me, "I always make it look as if I'm cleaning my knife."

But to pray in a public place is not the real problem. It is praying from the heart that is our problem, and we ought to begin by admitting to one another that we share this difficulty. Why do we imagine that others don't have the same problem we have? We need to confess that we have grieved the Lord, not only by the things we have done that we knew to be wrong, but by our unwillingness to spend time with him in prayer.

We need to confess to one another that our failure to pray as we ought is the reason we have failed God in so many other areas of our lives. Our failure to be in constant communion with the Lord has led us to live like spiritual cripples, not only lacking the power to do what is right, but afraid to take up the tasks that lie before us in a difficult and evil world. Perhaps there are some who are able to speak of their strength in these matters rather than their weakness. Let us rejoice with them and learn from them. But I suspect that there are more than a few of us who need to confess the opposite.

Fly now, pray later?

Not only do we pray too little, but we pray too late. We make the grave mistake of keeping our problems within ourselves, on the pretext that we do not want to "bother" the Father with our insignificant concerns. We think we ought to wait until something "really big" comes along. This is not the way of Jesus. When we look to the prayer life of Jesus, we find him demonstrating how vitally important it is to pray at the thresholds of life.

Jesus began his tasks with prayer. He did not look upon prayer as something to be used if needed. Each step along the way was prefaced with prayer. He teaches us that the time to be in conversation with the Lord is at any moment when there is a choice to be made, whether it is choosing a school, adjusting to a transfer to a new community and place of work, dealing with a doctor's diagnosis, or confronting some other new challenge to our faith. Not after we have tried and failed, but at the moment of first beginnings, is the time to pray. This was how Jesus ordered his life.

Strength through communion with God

It was always Jesus' practice to begin with prayer, but never did those prayers come from greater depths or rise to nobler heights than in those hours when he knew that his suffering and death were at hand. After his final, solemn moments with his disciples in the

Upper Room, Jesus went out and crossed the Brook Kidron, a winter stream in an otherwise dry ravine, and entered a quiet garden, there to pray. He could not carry out the task before him unless he prayed.

Therefore, when it is said that Jesus went off to pray to the Father, we should not take it to mean that Jesus took off on a casual little stroll down a garden lane for a conference with the chairman of the board about matters of mutual concern which he knew were already well in hand. His prayers came out of his genuine humanity, his need, his dependence. It is no small thing to hand yourself over to the hatred of the people around you, knowing that they will subject you to a cruel and certain death. This is how the letter to the Hebrews describes our Lord at prayer in those desperate times: "In the days of his flesh, Jesus offered up prayers and supplications, with loud cries and tears, to him who was able to save him from death, and he was heard for his godly fear" (5:7).

When we teach that Jesus began his task with prayer, we are saying that he began as an obedient Son entering into close and loving communion with the Father, for there was no other way to do what had to be done. If Jesus had merely said, "Understand prayer," he would have left us with a problem. Instead, he shows us how prayer can become an entrance into the presence of the Father. It is through the Father and our communion with him that we will find strength to take up our task.

Making a new beginning through Jesus

Seeing that Jesus began his task with prayer, how foolish we are to offer up the excuses we use to explain our lack of prayer: We don't think clearly in the morning. We are too tired at night. The children make too much noise. Above all, we are too busy, yes, *too busy* doing all the good things our Lord has given us to do!

Of course, in our better moments we may admit that such excuses do not address the real problem. Then we go on, "I know what I must do. I must set my house in order. Then I'll be able to enter into deep and meaningful communion with God." To which I say, "Don't hold your breath." For you are saying that somehow you must get to the point where you feel that you have at least become worthy enough to belong in the same room with God. This is not how it happens. Communion with God can begin only when you enter into his presence as a sinner assured and made bold through his gracious invitation. Communion with God begins as you tell him what's in your heart, hiding nothing (For who can hide anything from God?), and offering yourself to him as you are.

We need to begin the tasks of life in communion with the Father. The first step in doing that is to confess Jesus as our Redeemer and say with a thankful heart, "Jesus is my Lord, sent by the Father to save me, a lost and condemned person. Through him I am one with the Father." This confession must come from the heart, for the secret of prayer lies in admitting before the Lord that we have neither the strength nor the wisdom to do the things that need to be done. It isn't that God needs to be told what he ought to do. He already knows that. What he wants to hear from us is that we need him, for without him all our efforts will prove to be futile.

There is much good news for you and me in knowing how Jesus began his task. We are told that Jesus went to pray in a favorite place. It is good for us to find a special corner that becomes a place to pray. But even if we can't go off to pray, we can breathe the name of our Father, knowing that Jesus in his prayers has given us the assurance that we have the same heavenly Father looking down and listening with a loving heart.

Do you see your task? Then go to it! And as you do, turn to your Father with your every need. This is the way to begin your task.

A *prayer of beginning*

With you, O Lord, I shall begin my task; for when I invite you in, darkness becomes light, confusion is replaced by direction, and my empty soul is filled. Kneeling in weakness, I rise up in strength; sharing with you my burden, I am able to bear its weight. Give me, O Lord, your love and grace; this is all I need, all I ask, as I begin my task. Amen.

2

JESUS' PRAYER FOR OUR SPIRITUAL HEALING

Simon, Simon, behold, Satan demanded to have you, that he might sift you like wheat, but I have prayed for you that your faith may not fail; and when you have turned again, strengthen your brethren.

Luke 22:31-32

We sometimes hear the church likened to a mighty army. If this is so, then it is best to remember that we who belong to it are at all times to be counted among the walking wounded, for there is not a day in our lives when we do not come home bearing the marks of battle. What happened to Jesus happens to us. After Jesus was baptized in the River Jordan and the Holy Spirit had descended upon him, what came next? A life of spiritual ease? Not at all. It was then that he was "led by the Spirit" into the wilderness for a time of prayer and fasting, followed by the devil tempting him. Our life follows the same pattern. This is why our Lord's words to Simon are immediately recognized as words addressed to us as well: "Simon, Simon," Jesus said, "Behold, Satan demanded to have you, that he might sift you like wheat."

Sifted like wheat

The picture Jesus was creating is as follows: A farmer of ancient times stands next to his field that has been harvested. He holds in his hands a large sieve. He begins to shake it back and forth, slowly at first, then with ever increasing violence. The chaff blows away or falls to the ground. All that remains are the kernels of wheat, exposed and bare, ready to be carried away.

Although it may be that it is only in less developed cultures that wheat is still sifted in this manner, there is not a place on the globe where people are not being sifted by Satan in exactly that way. We all know the feeling. We find ourselves propelled this way and that in our little world. Then the shaking becomes more violent. We have no control over what's happening. We lie exposed and helpless, ready to be snatched up. We are the sifted ones.

Shaken by the enemy

Jesus spoke of this danger when Simon and the other disciples had gathered in the Upper Room for the Passover meal. Having issued the warning, Jesus then assures Simon that he has prayed for him. He prays for all of us, the sifted ones. He knows the enemy we face. His name is Satan. We may hesitate to talk about this enemy, but not Jesus. He knows better than anyone the power and intentions of this enemy. Having contended against him in the wilderness following his 40 days of fasting, he knew there was good reason to teach us to pray, "Deliver us from the evil one" (Matt. 6:13). Knowing the enemy's designs on the disciples, Jesus not only assured them of his prayers, but in their presence he prayed to the Father, "I do not pray that thou shouldst take them out of the world, but that thou shouldst *keep them from the evil one*" (John 17:15). Jesus took the power of this enemy seriously. He knew that if the first man and woman in all their reflected glory of the Maker could not withstand the cunning of this terrible adversary, how much more vulnerable would be his disciples of a later time.

Weakened by our flesh

Jesus understood why his disciples and all humanity have such difficulty when it comes to standing up against the adversary. He summed it up when he returned that night from his solitary vigil in the Garden of Gethsemane. He said to his well-intentioned but drowsy disciples, "Watch and pray. . . . The spirit indeed is willing, but the flesh is weak" (Matt. 26:41).

The flesh is not only weak; it is a willing conspirator. When Jesus talks about our "flesh," he is talking about that part of us untouched by the Spirit of God and, therefore, the source of our rebellion against God. It can be subjected, but it is never killed. It is a seed of destruction not unlike that known by an alcoholic who has been recovering for years, yet knows that the enemy is still within. Wiser than many nonalcoholics, he knows that if just one small opening is given, his enemy can seize control as if it had never been away.

By now we should have cut short any mistaken notion that the prayers of Jesus are offered in such a way that they weave a magic spell that will ward off the pressures applied by the evil one, the world, and our flesh. When Jesus told Peter that he had prayed for him, he did not say that this prayer would render Peter's fall impossible. That was Peter's responsibility. That was his battle to fight. We tend to forget it, but there is no such thing as spiritual repose while we let God fight our battles for us. God will give us his Spirit to fight our battles *with* us, but we always have a role in what happens or does not happen. This is what Jesus was talking about when he spoke of the man who got rid of an unclean spirit, but then remained empty within. Before long, the unclean spirit returned with seven other unclean spirits to make his condition even worse than it was at first. The enemy is always there, ready to counterattack.

Jesus knew the pressure-cooker world that awaited his disciples of that hour and of every age to follow. He knew that they would be subject to awesome times of sifting. He knew the temptations they would face. This is why he prayed that, while his disciples must be *in* the world, they might not be *of* the world—that world later warned against in the first letter of John: "All that is in the world, the lust of the flesh and the lust of the eyes and the pride of life, is not of the Father but is of the world" (1 John 2:16).

After the sifting, the turning

When Jesus prays for us, however, he does not dwell merely on our weaknesses. He also prays with great hope concerning our potential. Satan might demand to have us, but Jesus will not surrender us. This was the essence of his prayer for Peter. Knowing full well that his beloved but flawed disciple would soon taste defeat, Jesus offered hope even as he spoke of Peter's imminent fall. He told him that he was praying that his faith would hold fast in the aftermath of his sin. He reminded Peter that for God's children there is always the time for turning back again.

How flat and arid the Bible would be if its authors had withheld any account that would have shown the principal characters in a bad light. Thank God that they did not do that! Instead, through the chief apostle, who himself had to "turn again," we have the promise, "If I could come back, so can you!"

Not one of us could belong to God at this moment were it not for this word of hope from the lips of our

Lord, "And when you turn again. . . ." When does this happen? When we look to the account of how Peter denied his Lord, we find that it all began when Jesus turned first and looked at *him*. It was then that Peter left his place at the charcoal fire and retreated into the darkness. He paced back and forth, stopped, and then, resting his head against the courtyard wall, wept bitterly. Oh, the shame, the shame! Having boasted that he would die for his Lord, he had, at the first sign of pressure, denied him with an oath.

Turning again begins when we see that what we have been doing is destructive to our spiritual life, incompatible with being a follower of the Lord. It will be a time of remorse and perhaps even tears. We may feel that we are number one on the Lord's list of hopeless cases. "I knew what I was doing," a person laments, "but I did it anyway!" Friend, this does not make you unique. Everybody knows what he or she is doing. The excuse, "I didn't realize what I was doing," is a cop-out. It is not reality. But that is not yet the good news. The good news is that however disqualified we may believe ourselves to be, our feelings are not the last word. The last word belongs to God who speaks it through his Son, and by that Word qualifies the disqualified and declares worthy the unworthy. Yes, it was necessary for Peter to weep bitter tears; but when he turned again, he found life as he had never known it before.

After the tears, joy through the Spirit

It is at this turning point that the prompting of the Holy Spirit is so important. Therefore, we must make prayer a time for listening, not to ourselves as we repeat over and over what we have already said, but to what the Spirit has to say. Imagine visiting a doctor, telling him all your ailments, describing in detail every symptom, and then, before he can say a word, walking out of the office. Effective prayer provides space for solitude, which is far different than loneliness. It is withdrawal into the divine presence where the voice of him who is our Paraclete, Comforter, and Counselor, can be heard to say, "Go ahead, tell the Father all about it. Tell him that you know that you are sick and will die if not cured. Tell him that you are completely helpless and that only he can heal." This admission of helplessness is the first step into strength. Such helplessness is not despairing resignation. It is trust, simple and unadorned, that God in his mercy will accept us and love us.

It is the cross that makes our turning again the occasion for such joy. When we turn again, it is to see, as Peter saw, a Lord who has died upon the cross and risen from the dead, the everlasting sign of God's forgiveness and the promise of a new life. Have we turned away from him, denied him, loved the world too much, succumbed to the lust of the eyes and the pride of life? He knew it would happen. He knew he would be left alone, forgotten and forsaken by those who had pledged him their love. But he also knew that this forsakenness upon the cross would become the power of God to bring us back again, to stir up in us the hope that it is still possible to turn again. For his cross is the Father's pledge of total forgiveness and the promise that he always is waiting for us, ready to say, "Welcome home, my son! Welcome home, my daughter! Welcome home!"

A *prayer for spiritual healing*

Lift me up, Lord, from my fallen state; for there is no weakness but that which has been mine. Cheer

my heart with your word of love, and hold me fast
when my grasp grows weak.

I, the lost sheep who has been found,
the prodigal child welcomed home,
the wavering disciple called back,
the stained cloth of my humanity cleansed by your
blood,
through your prayer for my pardon, release, and
return,
cast out the chaff in my life,
that the wheat in me might be kept for life everlasting.
Amen.

3
JESUS' PRAYER OF SURRENDER

And they went to a place which was called Gethsemane; and he said to his disciples, "Sit here, while I pray." And he took with him Peter and James and John, and began to be greatly distressed and troubled. And he said to them, "My soul is very sorrowful, even to death; remain here, and watch." And going a little farther, he fell on the ground and prayed that, if it were possible, the hour might pass from him. And he said, "Abba, Father, all things are possible to thee; remove this cup from me; yet not what I will, but what thou wilt." Mark 14:32-36

A friend in the pastoral ministry showed me two picture cards he carries with him so he can give children a little present. One is a portrait of Jesus he likes very much. It portrays Jesus as a vibrant and vigorous young man, the shining look of an idealist in his eyes. The other pictures Jesus in the darkened groves of Gethsemane, kneeling in prayer, his eyes lifted up to heaven. My friend said that when he asks children which picture they would like, to his surprise they invariably pick the one of Jesus at prayer.

A need known to all

Why do they pick Jesus in Gethsemane? Perhaps they have an instinct that is common to both children and adults, an underlying awareness that the work Jesus came to do called for both suffering and prayer. We are, therefore, drawn to the picture of our Lord as he endures agony in the garden. Because this is what life so often comes down to, we feel our kinship with Jesus most deeply in those moments when we are scarcely able to breathe "Abba! Father!" and know how much we need to learn from him how to pray.

Entering the will of the Father

The first thing Jesus teaches us is that we must learn to enter into the will of the Father. As we observe him in Gethsemane, he had left behind the Upper Room and all the important things that happened there. It was time for solitude and prayer, and his beloved garden was the place for that. He had taken with him Peter, James and John, but then he drew apart from them a short distance. While the memory of the cup of blessing which he had held up before his disciples still was vivid in his mind, he saw before him another cup. It was not the cup of life but the cup of death. Deeply troubled in spirit, he fell to the ground and prayed, "Abba, Father, all things are possible to thee; remove this cup from me; yet not what I will but what thou wilt."

In order to understand the full depth and meaning of his entrance into the will of the Father, we must understand what Jesus was facing. Although he often had talked with quiet confidence about returning to the Father, death for him would involve much more than that. It always does. It was a time of testing. It was the time when Satan would make his last assault.

To me, it is most significant that one of the Gospels tells us that as Jesus prayed in Gethsemane, an angel appeared, strengthening him. The only other instance when angels came and ministered to him took place after Satan tempted Jesus in the wilderness and then departed. But, the Gospels report, Satan had not left for good. No, he only had "departed from him until an opportune time" (Luke 4:13). Satan is never done with us. He only bides his time. I believe that it was in Gethsemane that he saw that his "opportune time" had come. If so, then this time he would not offer the glitter of this world. No, this time he gleefully would make it ever so clear that Jesus would soon be tasting the fury and desolation of hell itself. For this is what lay behind the death Jesus was facing. He would be tasting for the whole world that death which is the wages of sin, the death that is separation from the Creator himself. But as terrible as this prospect was, and as much as Jesus drew back from it, he also looked beyond it and recognized that through this cup the Father would accomplish the salvation of all sinners. "Yes," his spirit said from within, "this is my will, too."

The prayer of acceptance

But the struggle was far from over. Jesus had to pray again. He had to be able to do more than say yes to the will of God. He had to learn to accept his role in carrying it out. So Jesus prayed a second time. This time he no longer prayed for the removal of the cup. It was clear that it had to be lifted to his lips. It would not pass unless he drank of it. He offered a prayer of acceptance. "My Father, if this cannot pass unless I drink it, thy will be done" (Matt. 26:42). It was then, we are told, that "his sweat became like great drops of blood falling down upon the ground" (Luke 22:44). Soon, so soon now, blood would flow, not merely from the pores on his brow, but from a thorn-crowned scalp, a wounded side, and pierced hands and feet.

Ready to take up the cross

Where were the disciples during this time of their Master's heart-rending prayer? They were there, but mostly sleeping. They awoke for a moment, and then dozed off again. But that's the way we humans are. We seldom learn much from watching others, even the very best, even Jesus. Only when we are thrown into our own crisis do we finally wake up to our need for the help of God.

Understanding them only too well, Jesus returned a third time, praying the same words, but not in an act of vain repetition. After this third prayer there was an air of resolve about him that was not there when he began to pray. He returned to the disciples filled with the power of the Spirit. He had agreed with the Father's will; he had accepted the cup he had to drink; and now he resolutely began to participate in the purposes of his Father. Gently nudging awake his sleepy friends, he said in a voice clear and steady, "Behold, the hour is at hand, and the Son of man is betrayed into the hands of sinners. Rise, let us be going; see, my betrayer is at hand" (Matt. 26:45). From that moment on he became a tower of strength, and there was no man alive who could break him.

Prayers in our own Gethsemane

As we listen to this threefold prayer of Jesus, it should become clear that each one of us has his or her own Gethsemane. The time comes when we stand alone. Friends may be nearby, but there is no one who really can stand with us. What a struggle it is to say, "Thy will be done," *for what is his will?* It's very hard to say yes to the will of God when our heart says, "No, this can't be his will!" It is tremendously important, therefore, to consider the question of what is God's will and what is *not* God's will.

A beautiful, loving, believing 15-year-old is killed, and we hear people saying, "Why did God take her?" I recall a very dear cousin of mine telling me with tears in her eyes how her 17-year-old son started off on a bike trip with two buddies. She kissed him good-bye, and said a little prayer. Twenty minutes later the three of them lay dead by the roadside, sideswiped by a drunken driver. People ask the same question, "Why did God take them?" Well, let's get it straight. Yes, God took them—to heaven. But it was a drunken driver, wantonly disregarding the will of God, who took their lives, not God.

However, it is precisely because there is evil at work in this world that we are called to pray the prayer of acceptance, and hold fast to the promise that the good and gracious will of God will prevail in the end. Even now, for those youngsters, life has overcome death. So in the name of Jesus we are able to pray, "Abba, Father, you have planted me in my own garden of Gethsemane. Help me to grow. Help me to bring forth good fruit through my faithfulness to thee." It is this spirit of acceptance that helps people hold on by means of one of the most dearly loved of all the promises in the Bible: "God is faithful, and he will not let you be tempted beyond your strength, but with the temptation will also provide the way of escape, that you may be able to endure it" (1 Cor. 10:13).

Now we are ready for the third stage in prayer. In the kingdom of God, commitment follows surrender. When Jesus says, "Rise, let us be going," faith replies, "Yes, Lord, I'm ready to follow you. Give me my cross."

Really? Can you really say that? It seems to me Peter once said that. "I will die with you, Lord. Though all the others may leave, I never will." But he did. The things we have been talking about are easier said than done, as we well know.

Our own "Abba, Father"

And so, I offer to you, as one of the greatest sources of hope and strength, the simple little beginning to the prayers Jesus offered. We've been talking about *what* he prayed, but just as important is *how* he prayed. In saying "Abba, Father," he was showing us how we can speak to God as a dear child speaks to a loving parent. *Abba* is the word Jewish children would use to address their father. It's like the word *daddy*. No prayer in all of Jewish literature ever records God being addressed in this way. It would have been considered too disrespectful. But Jesus did it, not to engage in childish chatter, but to show his deep and complete relationship with the Father.

The good news behind this for us is that through Christ we can pray with the same confidence, "Abba, Father." Through Christ we, too, are sons and daughters of the Father. We are encouraged to remember that on two different occasions (in Galatians 4 and Romans 8), the apostle Paul specifically declares that the Holy Spirit has been poured into our hearts to inspire us to say, "Abba, Father." Did we say earlier that there are times when you might feel able to say little more than "Abba, Father"? Well, good! That's exactly where you ought to begin, because that means you are talking to God as a child to a parent.

"Abba! Father!" These words are not a guarantee to us that there will be no sorrow, no questions, no times of terrible waiting, no cup of suffering, no cross in our lives. Nor will they automatically take us out of our own Garden of Gethsemane. But they will take us through Gethsemane and on to the cross, where we find in Christ the promise that there is one thing that he endured that you need never endure: the just retribution for our sin. He has taken care of that. He has borne it for us. We can say "Abba! Father!" with the full assurance that come what may, we are the forgiven children of God. We have a loving Father who will keep us in his care. So, in and through Jesus Christ, we find the strength to say, "Abba, Father, as you will!"

A *prayer of surrender*

O Father, my dear Father, who has taught me through your Son that I am most truly free when I lose my will in yours, help me to attain this perfect liberty by knitting my heart to yours. This I ask, knowing that I am worthy to be called your child only because of my kinship with my elder brother, your Son. I praise you, O Father, for it is you who have given to me this inheritance and sealed it with your own Spirit's inward call. In this my place of solitude and prayer, forgive me for what I have been, sanctify what I am, and lead me to seek no reward except the knowledge that I do your will. Amen.

4

THE ULTIMATE GOAL OF JESUS' PRAYERS

Now is my soul troubled. And what shall I say? "Father, save me from this hour?" No, for this purpose I have come to this hour. "Father, glorify thy name."

John 12:27-28

We have seen how Jesus began every task with prayer. We have heard him pray for our spiritual healing. We have witnessed him offer up his prayer of surrender in the Garden of Gethsemane. Somehow we can enter into those prayers more easily than the prayer before us at this moment: "Father, glorify thy name." The other prayers relate to a great need or testing in our lives, similar to the experiences of Jesus. But who feels a real need to glorify the name of our heavenly Father? Such a prayer does not come naturally, not anymore. If we are to offer it as we should, we will need to take a very close look at the subject of glory as Jesus prayed about it.

His prayer was put to the test

His prayer, "Father, glorify thy name," has been placed at this point in our series because one could say it was at the time of his arrest that it was truly put to the test. Upon his entry into Jerusalem Jesus had declared, "The hour has come for the Son of man to be glorified." Now in the garden, the torches of his enemies visible in the valley, he awakened his disciples and said with a sense of foreboding, "Behold, the hour is at hand, and the Son of man is betrayed into the hands of sinners" (Matt. 26:45). It was the prospect of this moment and the events to follow that had led him to say, a few days earlier, "Now is my soul troubled. And what shall I say, 'Father, save me from this hour'?" (John 12:27).

There was every reason for the thought to occur to him that perhaps he should ask to be saved from this hour. It was leading to death on a cross; and, as Bernard Ramm observes, "The cross is not a revelation of glory as the transfiguration was, but the *occasion* for glorification. It was not glorious in itself, but a bloody, painful, fearful, disgraceful mode of execution" (*Them He Glorified*, p. 41).

The fact that he knew what awaited him makes Jesus' resolve all the more significant as he answered his own question: "No, for this purpose I have come to this hour. Father, glorify thy name." He knew that the time had come to keep the divine appointment set by his Father. Nobody could advance that date, and no one could keep its hour from being struck. Jesus' prayer was the finalization of a decision made long ago when Satan took him to a mountaintop and offered him "the kingdoms of the world and the glory of them" (Matt. 4:8). Jesus had rejected that offer. The only glory he wanted was that which would come to the Father as the Father worked through him. This was all he asked, that he might glorify the Father by always obeying the will of the Father.

The kabod of God

The reason we have so much trouble with this prayer of Jesus is that we equate glory with fame. But

God doesn't need us to make him "famous." Jesus knew that. He knew that the glory of God is the sum of all his attributes, and that he is glorified when we show him as he is. This approach makes full use of the meaning of "glory" in the Hebrew scriptures, where it is known as *kabod*. The Old Testament scholar, Bernard Ramm, suggests the deeper meaning of this term as he explains that *kabod* is connected with weight, gravity, honor, fame, dignity, and splendor. The fact that God possesses these and similar attributes makes him "a God of *kabod*" (*Them He Glorified*, p. 10).

Jesus came to reveal that glory. "We beheld his glory," the evangelist began his prolog, "the glory as of the only Son from the Father" (John 1:14). He did not withdraw from the cross but saw it as the instrument whereby he would glorify the Father. With incredible boldness and confidence he followed up on his prayer with the prediction, "And I, when I am lifted up from the earth, will draw all men to myself" (John 12:32). He had already heard the promise that through him, the Father's name would be glorified yet once more, and now he predicted exactly what the Father would accomplish through his being lifted up on the cross. He would become an irresistible magnet who would draw countless people to the Father's love. He would be worshiped and praised as God's own sacrifice for sin, the Prince of Life who through his death has made possible the forgiveness of sin and everlasting life with God.

Through the cross the glory of God would be revealed in an act of grace that has no parallel in all of human history. "Yes," the Son says to the Father, "Glorify your name. Lift me high upon the cross! Lift me high that I, in turn, might lead all the world to you."

Our desire for glory

Surely this picture of the goal in Jesus' mind makes clear the nature of our mistaken search for glory. So often we have been like James and John, two of Jesus' closest friends. Only a few days before his death they came to him and said, "Grant us to sit, one at your right hand and one at your left, *in your glory*" (Mark 10:37). I wonder if in their minds there was also the question as to which of them would sit on his *right* hand, the position of power. One thing is certain. They wanted to be where everybody could see them! This is still our problem. When we think of glory, we think of fame—our fame.

When we speak of doing something for the glory of God, we somehow want to bask in the glow of that glory. A pastor is in the closing years of his career, and his church is engaged in a new building program. Suddenly he finds colleagues saying to him, "How about that? You'll be going out in a blaze of glory!" Is that what glory is all about? Is that our goal? Must we always fantasize, one way or another, about being in the center of some sort of ticker-tape parade? Must we always crave to be at the center of adulation and attention?

I believe that Jesus' simple prayer, "Father, glorify thy name," is at the same time a summons to each of us to look within and ask, "How much has my desire for glory allowed unhappiness to invade and take over my life, as I worry about whether or not I'm being properly recognized? How much time do I spend fretting over the extent to which my name is being glorified on the lips of others?"

Do not misunderstand the point being made here. I fully understand that we have been made to love and to be loved. I agree that it is important to give pleasure to those we love and, in return, find favor in their sight. A Christian is not called to deny or reject these human needs. In fact, the denial of these needs can lead to terrible spiritual damage. But a Christian knows that one's deepest joy comes from a sense of serving God and knowing his approval. It is this understanding that leads us to desire to pray in a new and better way.

Prayer with new priorities

Haven't we all dreamed at times of what this world could be like if it were filled with people who were praying, before anything else, that they might glorify God in their calling in the home and at the workplace? What changes in our lives might take place as prayer awakens a new awareness of the urgency in Jesus' words, "By this is my Father glorified, that you bear much fruit, and so prove to be my disciples" (John 15:8)? What might happen if the world were filled with people who were praying for the peace and good of the whole world? Who can begin to say what might be achieved to the glory of the name of God?

Make no mistake. Whatever our dreams, the real change must begin with us. An ancient prayer says, "Revive thy church, O Lord, beginning with me." Revive me, O Lord, by leading me to accept Jesus as the model for my life of prayer. That means praying as he did, that the Father's name be glorified, a goal that will take us beyond our frequently trivial petitions and lead us to a higher vision of the purposes of God.

Remember how Jesus said, "Now is my soul troubled"? We know the feeling, don't we? But shall we give in to despair? Shall we focus on the negatives in our lives? There is another option, and I invite you to put it to work beginning now. Form the habit of praising God in the midst of distress and darkness.

Engage in the regular practice, as Jesus did, of offering praise and thanksgiving for all that God is doing in your life.

Do you ask how? Here is an uncomplicated and time-tested suggestion. Say the doxology repeatedly: "Glory be to the Father, and to the Son, and to the Holy Spirit." Or, as you go about your business, breathe the little prayer, "Father, glorify your name through me." Such prayers do not require a formal "prayer time," but as we offer them throughout the day the glory of God will surround us and become a strong shield against every evil power.

As Jesus relied on prayer, so will you and I either rely on prayer or fall. When Jesus prayed that the Father's name be glorified, he received everything he needed to face his darkest and greatest hour: love, power, wisdom, and courage. It is all there for us, too, as we make Christ our dwelling place and adopt his way of prayer, saying with a new sense of commitment, "Father, glorify thy name."

A prayer that one's life might be a doxology

Teach me, Father, that your glory does not depend on my fame. Teach me instead that it shines most often and most clearly in the small duties of daily life carried out with faithfulness, humility, and cheerfulness. And if, dear Father, an extra measure of courage is required of me that I might face pain, shame, or death for your sake and for the glory of your name, lift me up and sustain me through the cross of your Son. Amen.

5

JESUS' PRAYER OF FORGIVENESS

Father, forgive them, for they know not what they do.

Luke 23:34

Albert Steinhaeuser turned to the scene of Christ's crucifixion with this reminder:

> The Passion of our Lord is not a pantomime, or mute spectacle, which we are left to interpret for ourselves. Accompanying the sufferings are the words of the Sufferer, in which their meaning is made known. As His death is the crown of His life, so His dying utterances are the crown and flower of all His sayings. The Seven Words on the Cross are the revelation of the inmost heart of the Savior (*The Man of Sorrows*, p. 188).

With that he turned to Jesus' first prayer from the cross, a prayer that perhaps is one of the most difficult for us to pray: "Father, forgive them, for they know not what they do."

An untapped power

The prayer of forgiveness is an untapped power in bringing about wholeness to our whole being. Father Robert DeGrandis gave an account of a woman who would not forgive her husband's girlfriend. The wife was suffering from arthritis that had crippled her, and the pain was excruciating. A nun who was praying with the woman finally helped her to see the necessity of forgiveness. The wife prayed, expressing her forgiveness of the other woman. Her pain disappeared and immediately she was able to get out of bed and serve refreshments to the nun and to another person who was present.

Father DeGrandis cited this as but one of many cases in which he has had a similar experience. He wrote, "We have seen cases where pain that was prayed for and did not at first go away, but when asked to forgive someone against whom the person held a grudge, the pain disappeared immediately as the person was articulating the forgiveness." In fact, he now always asks that people say a prayer of forgiveness before receiving the prayer of healing.

I too have had an experience of this sort following an act of reconciliation and forgiveness. Shortly after I had begun to serve in a new congregation, a very faithful member who had suffered greatly over the untimely death of the congregation's previous pastor let it be known that she found it absolutely impossible to receive any spiritual nurture from my ministry. When she would go to church, therefore, she would sit three pews in front of me and, when the sermon began, reach into the pew rack, pull out a Bible, and read it throughout the sermon. She explained to her friends that she just couldn't help it. She couldn't get a thing out of what I was saying and felt that all her nurture should come from God's Word.

For my part, I didn't know what to do. I would look in the mirror on a Sunday morning and ask myself, "Will she pull the same stunt today?" She would. I should have dealt with her more directly, but I didn't. Besides, I had my own problems. I was suffering from an excruciating pain in one of my arms whenever I served Holy Communion. It was so bad that by the time I finished the serving, I literally had to hold up with one arm the other arm that held the cup. Then one day, as the members were leaving, the woman who had been so distant took my hand and very quickly said, "I love you, pastor." With equal speed I replied fervently, "I love you" and named her name.

Whatever had been the cause of it, those hurried words of forgiveness and reconciliation removed the barrier that had stood between us. We both knew that. Some weeks later, I noticed that my arm didn't hurt anymore, and in thinking back, I realized that the pain had stopped following that exchange at the church door. I also noticed that she hadn't been reading the pew Bible during my sermons anymore.

Unmerited grace

It would be a grave mistake to think that these experiences teach that in every instance pain and sickness are caused by the absence of forgiveness. Life is not that simple. But it would be equally foolish to ignore the powerful effect the spirit of forgiveness can have on our mental and physical condition.

If the prayer of forgiveness is an untapped power, there is only one way to plug into it. We must turn to Jesus' own prayer of forgiveness and discover what it is actually saying to us. It is a prayer bringing to us the assurance of God's unmerited grace. It would be a mistake, therefore, to try to limit the breadth of this prayer by focusing on the words "they know not what they do," as if they mean that Jesus was making a distinction between excusable and inexcusable sins. He spoke those words as a part of his spirit of perfect compassion. He was not saying, "Father, ignore all this which is going on because, after all, they are ignorant."

He was not asking God to look the other way. He was asking for the forgiveness of people who were caught up in carrying out a terrible evil. As we hear Jesus pray, "Forgive them," let us always remember, when God forgives, it is always sin he forgives.

A great man once said, "At the foot of the cross, the ground is level." As we stand on this holy ground and hear Jesus' prayer for sinners, we know that there is no such thing as superior Christians who are in a position to look down on others. We must all look up to him as sinners standing in need of God's unmerited grace. There is no other way to live. A wealthy dowager archly said to a photographer, "I hope you do me justice." To which he replied, "Madam, what you need is not justice, but mercy." That is *my* story. That is *my* song.

Our story is the story of unmerited grace. Our song is the song of the wideness of God's mercy. This is always the point behind the best of Jesus' parables. In one of them he told of the young man who deliberately and totally wasted his inheritance. Alone in a far country, he heard a voice within himself saying, "Why don't you hurry home where you belong? Go home, claiming nothing, willing to be only a servant where once you were a son. But go home!"

The young man obeyed the voice. He turned toward home. Then while yet a great distance away, he saw, there on a hill, his father! "The waiting father," Helmut Thielecke called him. But not a waiting father for long. Because of this slightest turning, we see the father running down the hill, embracing him, clothing him, ordering a feast of joy on his son's behalf. Oh, the unmerited grace of the Father, our Father, ready always to receive us and deck us out with the fine cloth of his Son's own righteousness.

I believe that eventually each one of us, like that young man whose story Jesus told in Luke 15, comes to the point where we discover that the most awesome thing about God is his forgiveness and acceptance of sinners. Joy and peace come at last as we see that forgiveness is never *won*, neither by sufficient sorrow nor by a strenuous life of good works. That is how we humans operate: "Oh, sure, I'll forgive you, all right," we say, "but first you must prove you're really sorry." But not God. In the kingdom of God, forgiveness is always something that is *given*, not *won*. In the end, everything connected with God's forgiveness converges in the cross and his prayer, "Father, forgive them." Through his innocent suffering and death Christ offers the Father's own assurance that every sin will be forgiven. It doesn't make any sense that God should take such a risk with us, but that's why we call it grace.

Now for the hard part

It was Mark Twain, I believe, who said, "It's not the things in the Bible that I can't understand that bother me. It's the things I *can* understand that bother me." I know what he means, for Christ's prayer of forgiveness, which touches my needs, at the same time teaches me that I should pray for others with the same forgiving spirit.

Someone wrote a beautifully detailed portrayal of Christ telling his disciples to go to those who had wronged him, such as the guard who put a crown of thorns on his head, the crowd that cried for his blood, the soldier who thrust a spear into his side, and so on, to tell each of them that they were forgiven. But, as I see it, there is a sign of his forgiveness that is even more remarkable: that he returned to his disciples and restored them as his witnesses. I say that this is the more remarkable act because it has been my experience that it is often less difficult to forgive those who are one's avowed enemies; but when people you were really counting on have let you down, forgiveness comes hard.

Now comes the hard part. It is time to pray for the forgiveness of everyone in our lives. As strange as it may seem, that means offering up a prayer of forgiveness for oneself. We need to forgive ourselves and to ask God's forgiveness. How can we pray with a free and forgiving spirit for others if we are still in debt ourselves? Such a prayer is not to make excuses for our actions. It is to accept the grace of God in the name of Jesus. Free and forgiven, we can then move on to others.

When I ask people what sins are hardest to forgive, the most frequent responses are, "When someone has treated me very unfairly," or, "When someone I really counted on has let me down and betrayed my trust." Pray for them. Omit no one from your forgiveness. But as a friend of mine once said to me, "Don't try to do it all yourself. Ask God to bear the burden with you." Do this and a new power of forgiveness within your heart will follow.

Some of us may have so much forgiving to do that we hardly know where to begin. Some may have only one "burr under the saddle," one relationship where it seems impossible to practice forgiveness. Or we may deliberately have blotted from our conscious mind someone we should have forgiven. Whatever the situation, we all need to make a beginning somewhere, and the best place to begin is to follow Christ's example and say, "Father, forgive them."

It may not seem to be much of a prayer. The heart may not seem to be following the words. Offer it up anyway. Our trouble is that we make forgiveness depend too much on ourselves and our feelings. But forgiveness is first of all an act of the will regardless of our feelings. If we are worried about not having the right attitude, let this word from O. Hallesby be our encouragement:

> We feel that there is something God must see in us before He can answer our prayer. We think that He must find an earnest, urgent burning desire within us. . . . For this reason our prayers often become a soul-exertion by means of which we endeavor to produce within ourselves attitudes which will make an impression upon God. . . . He waits for only one thing, and for this He must wait, and that is for us to ask Him to help us (*Prayer*, p. 59).

With such a spirit of humility, let us ask God for help in establishing peace and reconciliation as he tells us to go about it. This, our Lord teaches us, is the way it works: Confess your faults to one another. Forgive one another. Pray for one another. Ask God's forgiveness for one another. Healing of all kinds— physical, mental, and spiritual—will follow.

Prayers of forgiveness

Purge my heart, O Father, of all bitterness, resentment, and desire for personal revenge against those who have failed me, hurt me, demeaned me, or acted in a spirit of enmity. Fully aware of my own imperfections, including my own most imperfect spirit of forgiveness, I boldly say in your name, I forgive them. I pray, O Father, that we who have need to be reconciled, one to the other, might see with one mind how you have laid our sin on the man Christ Jesus, who prayed for the forgiveness of us all. Begin among us this day that condition which shall prevail in heaven, where all souls are both forgivers and forgiven. In Jesus' name, I pray. Amen.

"Lord, do not hold this sin against them." (The prayer of Stephen when being stoned, Acts 7:60.)

6

JESUS' PRAYER INTO THE SILENCE OF GOD

My God, my God, why hast thou forsaken me?

Matthew 27:46

We may not care to talk about it very much, but many people have experienced what could best be called the silence of God just when they needed God most. They didn't expect it to turn out that way. They had been going along quite confidently, faithfully saying their prayers and finding them answered. But then, just when they needed most to hear from God, they heard nothing but silence. This is hard to take. Any of us can endure great trials if we can see a reason for our suffering. But when we find it necessary to say, "I just don't understand. I can't make any sense at all out of what is happening. How long must I wait?" then we know what it is to come up against the inscrutable silence of God.

Anybody out there?

Sooner or later such a sense of abandonment hits everyone. Jeremiah, Moses, the psalmists—they all felt this way. And then there was Jesus himself who cried out from the cross, "My God, my God, why hast thou forsaken me?" This pain-filled question hardly

43

sounds like a prayer, but it was; and in its own way it could be said to reflect the prayer of the human soul at its most profound and meaningful level of existence, the moment when it wonders if God really is out there after all.

These words of Jesus were a prayer because, in the first place, he drew them from the book of Psalms, which in Hebrew life was the prayer book in the home and the synagogue. They were like the words of a familiar hymn, beginning, "My God, my God, why hast thou forsaken me?" and then continuing, "Why art thou so far from helping me, from the words of my groaning? O my God, I cry by day, but thou dost not answer; and by night, but find no rest."

Many scholars believe that during his hours on the cross Jesus spoke this psalm in its entirety. If he did, it should be made clear that he was doing more than merely reciting the words of a hymn. He was making them his own in the most intense and personal way possible. With a breaking heart he is hurling them into the silence of God.

Humanity's derelict

As he addresses the silence of God, Jesus epitomizes the description of Psalm 22:1 as the "cry of dereliction." A derelict is something or someone abandoned, and this was the experience of Christ who, in praying this psalm, was for the first time giving it its full meaning. For many this is the greatest mystery the human mind can ever consider: to understand Matthew describing the Son of God as abandoned by the Father during that dark moment upon the cross. Yet this lone figure was without sin. He cried, "My God, my God, why hast thou forsaken me?" and heard no answer.

In that hour Jesus was humanity's derelict, abandoned and forsaken. However much you have felt alone, under whatever trying circumstances you have sent off a message but received no reply, nothing matches the Son's cry into the silence of God. Concerning the people of times gone by, the psalm says, "To thee they cried, and were saved; in thee they trusted and were not disappointed" (Ps. 22:5), but the Son of man must cry, "But I am a worm and no man" (Ps. 22:6).

Step by step, the very worst of the events written down in the psalm take place during Christ's crucifixion. The people pass by, mocking him, making faces at him, wagging their heads. Noting the silence of God, the mockers leap to the conclusion that Jesus is just one more liar or fool and taunt him: "He committed his cause to the Lord, let him deliver him, let him rescue him, for he delights in him" (Ps. 22:7-8, compare Matt. 27:39-43). His tongue cleaves to his jaw and he experiences a terrible thirst (Ps. 22:15, compare John 19:28).

Left alone except for a few grief-stricken, weeping women and one disciple, he must lament, "Yes, dogs are round about me; a company of evildoers encircle me; they have pierced my hands and my feet" (Ps. 22:16, compare John 19:18). As the final indignity, by the roll of the dice, "They divide my garments among them, and for my raiment they cast lots" (Ps. 22:18, compare John 19:23-24).

Why forsaken?

Why did all this happen to Jesus, the beloved Master about whom people so often exclaimed, "A teacher come from God!"? Jesus was the victim of injustice, cruelty, unbelief, and disloyalty. He was killed by the bigotry of some and the indifference of others. He experienced what God always experiences at the hands of a world filled with corruption. When human flesh is given the opportunity to accept or reject the things of God which are good and true, it turns away. We have all turned away. "All we like sheep have gone astray."

But there is more to it than that. Jesus' suffering was twofold. The *victim* of sin, he had at the same time become an *offering* for sin. In freedom he had willingly embraced the Father's plan from eternity that he should become the Lamb of God offered up for the sins of the world. He was more than a victim; he was the Father's very own instrument for the salvation of the world. The apostle Paul describes it succinctly: "For our sake he made him to be sin who knew no sin, so that in him we might become the righteousness of God (2 Cor. 5:21). The prophet Isaiah is more dramatic: "But he was wounded for our transgressions, he was bruised for our iniquities; . . . and the Lord laid on him the iniquity of us all" (53:5-6). Our Lord endured the awful silence of God so that ever after the Father might hear his cry for our mercy and pardon.

From despair to victory

As we consider all that Christ endured, and how he endured to the end, we begin to see in his prayer more than the cry of dereliction, as his words are usually described. We are hearing a prayer of magnificent courage. What shall one do when God himself seems to have joined that conspiracy that ignores one's cry for a just deliverance?

The drama, *A Man for All Seasons,* shows how Sir Thomas More dealt with this question. The former chancellor of England under King Henry VIII, he had resigned his office in opposition to the king's divorce and remarriage, followed by a break with the church in Rome. He refused to sign under oath a statement in which he would have approved what in his heart he believed to be absolutely wrong. For this he was imprisoned in the Tower of London, awaiting his execution.

His daughter visited him. She protested the injustice of it all: "In any State that was half good, you would be raised up high, not here, for what you've done already."

He replied, "But look now. . . . If we lived in a State where virtue was profitable, common sense would make us good, and greed would make us saintly. . . . But since in fact we see that avarice, anger, envy, pride, sloth, lust and stupidity commonly profit far beyond humility, chastity, fortitude, justice and thought, and have to choose to be human at all . . . why then perhaps we *must* stand fast a little—even at the risk of being heroes."

Meg protested again, asking if he hadn't done as much as God could reasonably want. He answered slowly, "Well . . . finally . . . it isn't a matter of reason; finally it's a matter of love" (Robert Bolt, *A Man for All Seasons* [Ontario: Scholastic Book Services, 1962], p. 81).

So it was for Christ. He should not have been hanging against a darkened sky. He should have been seated in Jerusalem's place of highest honor. But his was also a story of love, a love that would not let go. In this most desperate prayer he shows what was at the heart of his relationship to the Father. He would turn to no one but the Father, and to the Father he would turn at all times, even when there was silence.

In our study of Jesus' prayers on the way to the cross, a passage from the letter to the Hebrews has shown itself to have recurring significance: "In the

days of his flesh, Jesus offered up prayers and supplications with loud cries and tears, to him who was
able to save him from death, and he was heard for
his godly fear. Although he was a Son, he learned
obedience through what he suffered; and being made
perfect he became the source of eternal salvation to
all who obey him" (5:7-9).

All this has happened. His loud cry, "Why have
you forsaken me?" *was* answered. The answer came
through the resurrection. Because of his suffering and
redemptive love, the Father has raised up his Son and
given to him the power to fulfill his promise of eternal
salvation and the coming of the Holy Spirit to dwell
in our hearts.

New and great hope is offered to us through the
victory already gained by Christ. Our faith may seem
to be totally dormant, like a seed lying in the ground.
But that waiting itself may be a time of preparation
for the bursting forth of the life of the risen Christ
within our lives, replacing what perhaps has been
nothing more than surface Christianity. That is how
growth so often happens. When we think we are
doing nothing and are caught in the silence, the Lord
begins to work through his Spirit.

Because Christ's prayer has been answered, we
have assurance that, even though we seem to be surrounded by silence, we shall never pray alone again.
By the power of his risen love we have within us "the
Spirit himself [who] intercedes for us with sighs too
deep for words. And he who searches the hearts of
men knows what is in the mind of the Spirit, because
the Spirit intercedes for the saints according to the
will of God" (Rom. 8:26-27). In those moments when
we feel compelled to ask, "Why have you forsaken
me?" he who first asked that question calls on us to
reflect on this passage from Romans, or upon his
many promises that he would not leave us comfortless

but would send to us the Holy Spirit, he who would be our constant companion.

Anyone who serves in the ministry knows that the "whys" of life never go away. They are always reappearing among God's people in yet another form. Joined to Christ, however, we can know that even as we ask "Why?" God is there. He is listening and he will answer.

Prayer verses for times of silence

"Out of the depths I cry to thee, O Lord! Lord, hear my voice!" (Ps. 130:1-2).

"Even the darkness is not dark to thee, the night is as bright as the day" (Ps. 139:12).

"Whoever comes to me I will in no wise cast out" (John 6:37).
"We are afflicted in every way, but not crushed;
perplexed but not driven to despair;
persecuted but not abandoned,
struck down, but not let to die,
always carrying in our body the death that Jesus died, so that the life that Jesus lives might also reveal itself in our mortal bodies" (2 Cor. 4:8-10 [composite translation]).

I am but an earthen vessel, O Lord, an easily crushed Styrofoam cup. Hold me gently in your fingertips and fill me once again. I am so empty without you. Amen.

7

JESUS' PRAYER FOR OUR ONENESS

I do not pray for these only, but also for those who believe in me through their word, that they may all be one.

John 17:20-21

"Because there is one bread, we who are many are one body, for we all partake of one bread" (1 Cor. 10:17). With these words, the apostle Paul gives expression to the fellowship that God creates at the Lord's table, a present reality that always is in need of future fulfillment. It was for this oneness that Jesus prayed when he drew his disciples about him at Passover, sharing with them in the Upper Room a last supper. It was a prayer for oneness among those who would be his disciples, both then and now.

Called to his table of love

The room had grown ever more quiet as the evening wore on. The disciples were not at all prepared for what Jesus would say and do; quite likely the beginning of the meal had been marked by noisy greetings and excited speculation as to what might soon be taking place at the coming of the kingdom of God. Their state of preparedness was not unlike ours as we

gather in church to hear the words of Jesus and partake of his supper. We come in a rush, almost late.
We pause to pass on a quick message to a friend we
had been trying to reach. We find that it takes a good
deal of effort to tune in to words of confession and
praise, so unlike anything we have been using
throughout the day. It takes time to settle down.

It was like that for the disciples. Slowly the nature
of the events that were about to take place began to
sink in. They watched with quiet amazement as Jesus
knelt before each one of them, solemnly washing their
feet in an act of servanthood. As they sat at the table
they heard him speak mystifying words about how
one of them would betray him. Some heard him say
softly to Judas, "What you are going to do, do
quickly." A sense of terrible foreboding is conveyed
as John's Gospel goes on to say of Judas, "So, after
receiving the morsel, he immediately went out; *and it
was night*" (13:27, 30).

To those who remained Jesus spoke quietly and
earnestly. He spoke of the sorrow that must come
before they could know joy. He spoke of his closeness
to them and called them, not servants, but friends.
He promised that though they would be scattered,
they would not be alone. He would send to them the
Holy Spirit. With such words he comforted and
strengthened them.

Then he prayed. Jesus had not composed this
prayer in the isolation of a private study. It came from
the chambers of his soul. He prayed that the Father
might be glorified through him. He prayed, not that
they would be taken out of the world, but that they
would be kept safe from the evil one, supplications
about which we have already spoken. But above all,
his prayer that night is remembered for the words, "I
do not pray for these only, but also for those who
believe in me through their word, that they may all

be one; even as thou, Father, art in me, and I in thee" (John 17:20-21). So heartfelt was his desire that he repeated his petition, praying "that they may be one even as we are one, I in them and thou in me, that they may become perfectly one, so that the world may know that thou hast sent me and hast loved them as thou hast loved me" (John 17:22-23).

Oneness through the indwelling of Christ

This is not the oneness of a sentimental love feast or a gathering of friends expressing the comradeship they find in some particular cause or game. Nor does he pray that we might all become the same. He is not the master cookie cutter in the kingdom's kitchen. Jesus prays instead for that oneness that will reflect the unity of the Godhead itself, a unity of spirit and purpose even while there is a multiplicity of gifts and functions. This is an enormous prayer. It speaks of a goal so high that we wonder how we might even dare to speak of it. For we know that even when we gather together in one room we are still much more like scattered seeds than one loaf.

If we would experience such unity, the first thing to note is that Jesus does not pray that we shall find it through an imitation of the oneness of the Father and the Son. He knows that the act of imitation is an effort to reach a goal through our own strength and power, and is bound to fail. The oneness for which Jesus prays can come only through our participation in him, a participation uniquely experienced in the supper he has given to us, saying, "This is my body. . . . This is my blood." This oneness does not begin with what we do. It begins with what Christ does. It is a unity that begins with his indwelling. Let the oneness of his disciples exist, he prays, in the only way that really matters: because he is in them even as the Father is in him.

Is such oneness possible for us? It is, but only if we understand that we are not to remember the meal, as holy as it is, but to remember Jesus. We have been invited to this table in order to recall that act of love in which his body and his blood were given and shed for us in that awful and lonely death on Calvary. It was there that he brought about the reconciliation of the people of this earth with their Creator, for "in Christ God was reconciling the world to himself, not counting their trespasses against them" (2 Cor. 5:19). When we hear his prayer "that they also may be in us. . . . I in them and thou in me" (John 17:21, 23), we must never forget that the voice belongs to none other than the Son of Man who made such unity possible through his own sacrifice upon the cross.

Our oneness with each other

In our coming together we are aware of the Christ who has come to be with us. But, in remembering, we are stirred to a new awareness of one another. In remembering, we find not only reconciliation with God but with one another. It must be so, for one's salvation is never lived out in isolation. Our new life from God is always corporate as well as personal. Jesus prayed for such oneness because he knew that this unity would be living proof to the world that he has been sent by the Father: I pray "that they all may be one . . . that the world may believe that thou hast sent me" (John 17:20, 21).

In the Lord's Supper our new life "hid with Christ in God" becomes a life of solidarity with our brothers and sisters who are fellow members of the body of Christ. In this meal we are making a first step in giving expression to what Jesus has already brought about: the creation of a new people of God out of an alienated human race. It was of this new creation, to which we now belong, that he also spoke when in that Upper Room he prayed: "I glorified thee on earth, having accomplished the work which thou gavest me to do" (John 17:4).

The new creation is in place, but its completion is far from done. So that we might know how to pray with our Lord that this new creation might become more what it ought to be, there are some questions we first need to ask ourselves: What is it that binds us to one another? To those of other faiths? To the departed? What outlook will help us be instruments for realizing a oneness with others who do not share our background, interests, and beliefs? Many answers could be given, but there is one special picture that emerges from the very room where Jesus had assembled his disciples around his table of love. He said to them, "I am the vine, you are the branches" (John 15:5). Prayers for oneness which envision all of us attached to that one true vine can have a powerful and positive effect.

A *oneness that never ends*

One day a pastor decided to take his little boy with him as he brought Holy Communion to an elderly shut-in. She lived in a snug log cabin at the center of a small woods. The inside walls were wood paneled, and the chairs and table were highly polished pine. They sat at the table as the pastor took the bread and wine from his communion kit and administered the sacrament. The little boy sat very still. When the final prayers had been said, the delicate fingers that had taken hold of the body of Christ reached into her own treasure box. She brought out a gingerbread cookie and gave it to the little boy. She smiled, and he smiled back. "Thank you," he said. They left then, and as they walked away from the cabin, the father wondered at the oneness that had been expressed in that little room.

The little boy is a grown man now, a pastor himself. He is my son. The frail lady is in heaven. But the story of their oneness is not over. He who prayed for our oneness also said, "Father, I desire that they also, whom thou has given me, may be with me where I am, to behold my glory which thou hast given me in thy love for me before the foundation of the world" (John 17:24). We, who through his saving name have become his saints below, shall by that same grace become his saints above, there to dwell at last in perfect and eternal unity. There we shall break bread together with the Lord. His new creation, this fellowship divine, will never end. This is his prayer for us. This is his promise. We can count on it.

A *prayer for oneness*

Help me to remember, O Lord, that I am the branch, you the vine. As I look around in my church and see other branches, let me never forget that we are all attached to that same vine, recipients together of the life that you give to us and the fruit you produce through us. Take me beyond religion as a private affair, reminding me that in calling me to yourself you have put me down into the midst of a family, a household, a colony, a flock. I thank you for my sisters and brothers. I commit myself to them, knowing that in them I shall find you. Amen.

8
JESUS SHOWS US HOW TO DIE

Then Jesus, crying with a loud voice, said, "Father, into thy hands I commit my spirit!"

Luke 23:46

One Friday several years ago Joseph LaLond, a 17-year-old boy in a congregation I served, took his mother aside and said to her, "Mom, I want you to know that if anything ever happens to me, you can be sure that I am going to heaven." He told her of his faith in Jesus. He was very explicit about his faith in this conversation. The next Monday, while working at the local lumber yard, a forklift fell on him and killed him instantly. But before he died, he had left his mother with no doubt about whether he knew how to face death.

Who cares?

More recently Stephanie Radvan, a 15-year-old member of our congregation, was killed. She was coming home from a youth fellowship when the car in which she was riding was struck by a drunken driver. In going through her room her mother and father found a piece written shortly before her death. She had written:

"What's wrong with society?

"People don't care, or if they do, it's for the wrong reason. They go to church and know there's a God, but they don't care.

"Picture this: A husband comes home from work and turns on the news. The anchorman, say Dan Rather, is saying (all the while smiling) 'We had another killing today and here is Joe Smith reporting on this tragic circumstance.'

"The husband yawns and calls to his wife who is in the kitchen baking bread, 'There was another person murdered today.'

"The wife, totally disinterested, calls back, 'That's nice dear. That makes 722 this week.'

"What's wrong with this picture? The husband didn't care and neither did the wife.

"Now let's look at the same picture with a slight change.

"The husband comes home from work and turns on the news. The anchorman reports a murder. The husband yawns and tells this to his wife. The wife says, 'That's nice' and then asks if he saw their son coming home from work. The husband replies, 'No. Should I have?'

"The wife stops working and comes into the family room where the husband is watching TV. She says, 'He didn't come home from school today.'

"Now, tell me what's wrong with this picture? It's the same as the other one, but will they still not care when they find out that it was their son who was killed while coming home?"

Along with a conclusion to that piece that affirmed, "God is there and he cares," they found other little notes and plays that showed her closeness to God.

The things that really matter

Both these young people were led by the Lord to come to grips with something most of us avoid: the reality of death. They possessed an awareness of their own mortality which is woefully lacking in many adults, who act as if they need never think about such things. The young woman had thought about them. She knew that death was more than a statistic. It is the end. She wrote that it is a time for meeting God, a time when it will be revealed whether or not one's life has centered around the things that matter.

The things that matter. Recalling these young deaths sent me to my notes of bygone years, and I found something I had completely forgotten: my notes from my early years of ministry in Detroit of a man who had lost a beautiful young daughter of 15. He leaned back in his chair at our congregational meeting one evening and smiled a slow, sad, half-smile, and said, "You guys—you guys sit here all night arguing, and you don't even know what really matters."

The thing that matters is whether we really know how to die. And don't think that there will be time for a special cram course right at the end. Now is the time. Now is the time to consider whether we are ready to say with Jesus those words that were both his last prayer and final words: "Father, into thy hands I commit my spirit."

Long after all our stocks and bonds and policies have turned to yellowed dust; long after all the desires that now consume our waking moments are gone; long after all the structures of this world have become fallen ruins; long after all the trains and buses have stopped running, planes flying, and rockets orbiting; long after all these things have become at best "misty, water-colored memories"; the one thing that will matter will be whether we knew how to pray, at the end, "Father, into thy hands I commit my spirit."

The prayer to the heart of the Father

Do you know how to do that? Do you care about knowing how to do that? Stephanie wrote, "God is there and he cares. So why can't we?" Do we care whether we ourselves, those we know and love, and others whom we do not know, know both how to live and how to die? For isn't this why the Prince of Life came to die on Good Friday, the darkest of all days in the history of humankind, that we might all be able to say with him, "Father, into thy hands I commit my spirit"?

"Father!" We must have addressed God thousands of times as "our Father" as we've recited the Lord's Prayer; but when Jesus taught us so to pray, he was doing more than suggesting a comfortable way to begin a prayer. He was offering the foundation for an entirely new and lasting relationship with God. The full meaning of what he was teaching us in those words came about when he offered that prayer on the cross. As he died, that prayer was his personal promise to us not only that God was his "Abba, Father," but that through him we could, with complete confidence, say those words *with* him.

Let me tell you how this can be so for you by telling you what Jesus came to do and how he did it.

No one ever experienced a greater darkness of soul than Jesus did as he hung upon the cross; but he died as he lived, and that little prayer he offered in death was the prayer he had offered in life. It was the prayer that every Jewish child offered at bedtime, one found in Psalm 31. As an evening prayer, it was a prayer preparing oneself for life, not for death. It was a looking forward to the coming morning and the Lord being present as one's rock and fortress, guide and protector, providing help against every enemy of body and spirit.

If ever there lived a good man who proved that as we have lived and prayed, so we will die, it was Jesus. He took that little prayer and added that brief preface which amounted to his own personal signature, "Father!" He then proceeded to show that although everyone around him considered him to be smitten by God and afflicted, he *knew* that the time was coming when the Father's love would be revealed and he would be completely vindicated.

Jesus died as the true representative of what a human being ought to be. He died trusting that God was his Father, not requiring the absence of pain to prove it, not demanding that there be an immediate reward for his faithfulness or else he would revert to unbelief. He simply kept focused on the one thing that mattered: the promise of his Father that he loved him and would glorify him. He believed in what could not yet be seen; and it was this trust that made him, as the letter to the Hebrews puts it so beautifully, "the pioneer and perfecter of our faith, who for the joy that was set before him, endured the cross, despising the shame, and is seated at the right hand of God" (Heb. 12:2).

Because of his faithfulness to the promise set before him, his crucifixion has become the world's salvation. Having been tempted in every respect as we are, yet without sin, he has now become the new Adam, who has succeeded where the first Adam failed. The apostle Paul would later put it this way: "As one man's trespass led to condemnation for all men, so one man's act of righteousness leads to acquittal and life for all men" (Rom. 5:18). By faith you can claim that Christ's righteous deed upon the cross was for *you*. By faith you can choose to die with Jesus and be buried with him. By faith you can rise with him and walk in newness of life.

The way to go

Do you know how to die? More than we care to acknowledge, as we have lived, so we shall die. The truth of this axiom is demonstrated in the life of Dietrich Bonhoeffer, a profound theologian and yet humble seminary professor. Refusing the safety he could have found outside of his native Germany, his resistance to Adolf Hitler eventually led to a military prison. There he became a rock to his fellow prisoners. Respectful guards secretly began to bring him to other cells to minister to despairing prisoners. He showed them all that in life as well as in death it is possible to say, "Father, into thy hands I commit my spirit."

On April 8, 1945, after conducting a little service for his fellow prisoners in which he preached on the text, "By his wounds we are healed," the end came for him. Payne Best, a British officer who was there, wrote in *The Venlo Incident*, "He had hardly finished his last prayer when the door opened and two evil-looking men in civilian clothes came in and said, 'Prisoner Bonhoeffer, get ready to come with us!' These words, 'Come with us' had come to mean one thing only—the scaffold. We bade him good-bye—he drew me aside, 'This is the end, but for me the beginning of life' " (from Eberhard Bethge's sketch in *Psalms: The Prayer Book of the Bible*, by Dietrich Bonhoeffer [Minneapolis: Augsburg, 1974] pp. 83-84).

"Father, into thy hands I commit my spirit." In his dying, Bonhoeffer reflected the confidence found in Jesus' last prayer, a confidence this Christian martyr expressed in a poem he had written about death as "the highest feast on the road to eternal freedom" (*Last Letters of Resistance*, Fortress, 1986). It ended,

"Freedom, how long we have sought thee in discipline, action,
   and suffering,
dying, we now behold thee revealed in the Lord."

There's an old saying, "true repentance is never too late, but late repentance is seldom true." The thief—or more accurately, the terrorist—who refused to see in Jesus hope for himself at this moment of judgment—is the rule. The man who at the last moment of death turned to Jesus is the exception. But there is always time for one more exception. There is time right now to tell Jesus that you know him as the Son of God who has shown you how to live and, therefore, how also to die.

A *prayer at life's ending*

O Father never sleeping, as I draw near to this life's last night, keep me ever mindful that darkness and light are as one to you. What I, as a stranger in exile here on earth, have seen only from afar but have believed, open now to me through the promise of your Son. Make wide for me the gates to life and receive me into your everlasting joy. In the name of Jesus. Amen.

9

HE LIVES TO PLEAD
FOR ME ABOVE

But Mary stood weeping outside the tomb, and as she wept she
stooped to look into the tomb; and she saw two angels in white,
sitting where the body of Jesus had lain, one at the head and
one at the feet. They said to her, "Woman, why are you weeping?" She said to them, "Because they have taken away my
Lord, and I do not know where they have laid him." Saying
this, she turned round and saw Jesus standing, but she did not
know it was Jesus. Jesus said to her, "Woman, why are you
weeping? Whom do you seek?" Supposing him to be the gar-
dener, she said to him, "Sir, if you have carried him away, tell
me where you have laid him, and I will take him away." Jesus
said to her, "Mary." She turned and said to him in Hebrew,
"Rabboni!" (which means Teacher). Jesus said to her, "Do not
hold me, for I have not yet ascended to the Father; but go to
my brethren and say to them, I am ascending to my Father
and to your Father, to my God and to your God." Mary
Magdalene went and said to the disciples, "I have seen the
Lord"; and she told them that he had said these things to her.

John 20:11-18

Looking for a dead Christ

The Gospel of John focuses on one of the women
who had gone to the tomb of Jesus. Her name was

Mary Magdalene. She had gone to the tomb with only
one thing in mind. She wanted to show her love for
her dead master by anointing his body with spices.
She approached the tomb the way many people go
to church today. They want to pay their respects to
Jesus, but they consider him to be a part of the past,
a man who belongs to the company of the dead.

After discovering the tomb to be empty and running to tell Peter and another disciple, Mary found
herself again outside the tomb, still alone, and weeping bitterly. She looked inside the tomb again, and
this time saw two angels sitting where the body of
Jesus had lain, one at the feet and one at the head.
Barely able to see them through her tears, she heard
them ask, "Why are you weeping?" "Why do I
weep?" she responded. "Why, as if what has happened isn't bad enough, they have also taken away
my Lord and I don't know where they have laid him."
Her answer revealed that she considered Jesus dead,
and that's that. What bothered her was that she
couldn't pay her last respects.

Yes, that seemed to be the reason for her weeping, at least on the surface. Or did one little word
suggest something beneath the surface? She referred
to Jesus as "my Lord." There was a hint of the same
despair that was expressed by two other disciples on
the road to Emmaus. They said, not realizing that they
were talking to the risen Jesus, "We had hoped that
he was the one to redeem Israel" (Luke 24:21). Yes,
for a little while there had been a glimmer of hope
that Jesus was much more than any other man who
had walked the face of the earth; but Mary had given
up on all that now. She asked for nothing more than
the dead body of Jesus.

If the angels had planned to say more, she didn't
give them a chance. She turned away from them; and
as she did, she found herself looking at Jesus himself,

though she didn't know it. This shouldn't surprise us. The last thing she was looking for was a living Jesus. So Jesus asked Mary, exactly as the angels had, "Woman, why are you weeping?" And he added, "Whom are you seeking?" She gave the same answer. She was looking for something she would never find. She was looking for a dead Christ; and he couldn't be found, for he is not dead. He is alive.

What happened to Mary still happens to people. At one time they placed such high hopes in Jesus. They really counted on him. They talked about the salvation he offered them. But then for some reason, that hope was smashed. Now they say, "I hoped in him—once. But something went wrong. They took my Lord away, and I can't find him any more, try as I will." Maybe it was an experience in school, or in a war, or at home, something that left Jesus a dead Lord. If they could, they would weep for him, inwardly if not outwardly. Within their hearts they know they have lost a friend, or even more than a friend.

Visited by a living Lord

Next something very interesting happened. For all of Mary's longing to find Jesus, it was not she who found him, but Jesus who found her. Remember how he once said that he is the good shepherd who knows his sheep by name, and that his sheep know his voice and come to him? Well, then he spoke Mary's name, just as at this moment he speaks your name, no matter how far you have been wandering from his fold. When she heard her name, she answered. So can you. She said, "Rabboni!" or "Teacher!" She was on her way. She knew he was alive instead of dead. But she still had a way to go before faith would take hold. She was speaking only of what he had been, not what he had become.

When in her joy she grasped him, she heard him make it very clear that he wanted the action in progress to be broken off. Literally translated, he said, "Cease touching me," or "Do not keep clinging to me." He had to ascend to the Father. He was now the exalted Lord, and Christian life was going to be more than hanging onto a living visible, audible, tangible Jesus. A revived "Teacher" was no more the answer to her search than that lifeless corpse she was looking for at first.

Robert H. Smith sums up the essence of Jesus' message beautifully: "I, the one standing here talking with you and touched by you, being in this form and fashion, am not the one with whom Christians have to do; this manner of contact is not the goal" (*Easter Gospels* [Minneapolis: Augsburg, 1983], p. 164).

The *goal* is to have that faith which accepts Jesus as the exalted Christ who has risen from the dead and ascended to the Father as the victorious Son of God. We have been reflecting on Jesus' prayers as he went toward the cross. More than once we have seen how that journey could be summarized in this surprising and thought-provoking little verse from the letter to the Hebrews: "In the days of his flesh, Jesus offered up prayers and supplications, with loud cries and tears, to him who was able to save him from death, and he was heard for his godly fear" (5:7).

Yes, Jesus prayed with loud cries and tears, too. But the Father vindicated him, and through his victory he offers us an entirely new outlook on the hope that is before us and the whole world. Why stand weeping at the graveside of worn-out bodies and shattered dreams? "I am your Redeemer, and I live!" he tells us.

The apostle Paul made the same point to some wavering Christians at Corinth. "If Christ has not been raised, then your faith is a delusion and you are still lost in your sins. It would also mean that the believers in Christ who have died are lost. If our hope in Christ is good for this life only, and no more, then we deserve more pity than anyone else in the whole world" (1 Cor. 15:17-19 TEV).

This is logic at work, terrible but unanswerable logic. A dead Christ cannot give life to those who died in him. But Christ is not dead. The apostle continues with great joy, "But the truth is that Christ has been raised from death, as the guarantee that those who sleep in death will also be raised" (1 Cor. 15:20 TEV).

Who can be against us?

It's a simple hymn but so direct and down-to-earth. "I know that my Redeemer lives! What comfort this sweet sentence gives!"

Why do we weep?

> He lives to silence all my fears;
> He lives to wipe away my tears.

Why think there is no one to help us as we face our troubles of the day? He lives and enables us to say with Paul in his letter to the Christians at Rome, "If God is for us, who is against us? He who did not spare his own Son but gave him up for us all, will he not also give us all things with him?" (Rom. 8:31-32). Who can accuse us, condemn us, frighten us, or threaten us? We have Christ Jesus who not only died for us, but is today our living Lord "who was raised from the dead, who is at the right hand of God, who indeed intercedes for us?" (Rom. 8:34).

Yes, the letter to the Hebrews echoes, Jesus "continues forever. Consequently he is able for all time to save those who draw near to God through him, since he always lives to make intercession for them" (Heb. 7:24-25).

> He lives to bless me with his love;
> He lives to plead for me above;
> He lives my hungry soul to feed;
> He lives to help in time of need.

He lives above to intercede for us below. This sums up his priestly vocation. And how does he pray for us? On our behalf he prays for everything that he asked on behalf of his disciples while he was with them here on earth. He prays that we will be given the Holy Spirit. He prays for our oneness with all members of the body of Christ. He prays that our lives will be filled with the fruits of the Holy Spirit as we grow in faith and love. He prays that we might have strength to withstand the temptations of the evil one. He prays that if we, like Mary Magdalene, came to this moment expecting only to pay our proper respects to the dead, then we may also, like her, find that it is time to go on to something new and better. He prays that we will ask for the coming of the Father and the Son and the Holy Spirit to make their home in us, just as he promised.

Our Redeemer is not dead. He lives. We can speak to him. We can breathe his name in an almost wordless prayer, and as we do, we will find him who is above coming to dwell with us below. We will find him coming to us through that prayer with a power we never imagined possible. We will find him becoming a source of strength, paralyzing the forces of evil and quickening our faith (Rom. 7:24-25).

As we conclude our consideration of the prayers of our crucified and risen Lord, let us offer together within our hearts this prayer of praise: "I know that my Redeemer lives. He lives to plead for me above."

A *prayer to our living Lord*

O Jesus, mystery divine, ascended to the Father that you might be with us through the coming of the promised Comforter, even the Spirit of truth, fill us with a sense of your presence.

O Jesus, living Lord, whose kingly face the angels now see, stay with us and teach us to pray as you have prayed.

O Jesus, advocate with the Father, pray for us, that our sins be forgiven and a new life opened to us, beginning now and never ending. Amen.

10

WHAT WE HAVE LEARNED

Sister Miriam Murphy, a good friend, a great spiritual leader at the Center for Continuing Education at Princeton Theological Seminary, and the author of a most helpful book, *Prayer in Action,* once said to me, "Most people don't drown their fears. They give them swimming lessons." She is right on target. Everyone knows what it is like to be deeply troubled. The difference among people lies not in the feelings they experience, but in what they do with them.

Most people, when they drift away from worship and prayer, do not do so because they have set themselves against God, but because something has not worked right for them. They have become discouraged. They are troubled. They feel they've lost touch with God. They don't see how they can get things going again. They have given up trying.

Now we have seen that there is another way. We have seen the possibilities that open up when one offers up the prayer that fell first from the lips of Jesus: "Abba! Father!" In so speaking he introduced to the people of God a new dimension in prayers to God. It is a prayer we may say with him. It is a prayer said in communion with Christ by which we are moved to turn to God as our Father, telling him with an open heart about every need, fear, or hope, thereby reaching the state of spirituality described by Paul when he wrote, "When we cry, 'Abba! Father!' it is the Spirit himself bearing witness with our spirit that we are children of God, and if children, then heirs, heirs of God and fellow heirs with Christ, provided we suffer with him in order that we may be glorified with him" (Rom. 8:15-17).

Words such as *prayer, trust,* and *endearment,* have often served only as salt in the wounds of those who have become discouraged and troubled. Through our study of the prayers of Jesus, however, we have come to realize that a sense of inadequacy, an inability to know what can be done with your problems, or a feeling that we don't even know what to ask for, or how to say it, does not mean that all is lost. In fact, this may be the best thing that can happen to us because now we are ready to turn to God in the one way that matters: giving everything over to him. It is then we are ready to pray.

In the prayers our Lord offered on the way to the cross, we are shown repeatedly that prayer is more than knowing how to put together a proper combination of words. Prayer is an attitude, and the development of one's own prayer life should be a never-ending process. If we would have the prayers of Christ become our own, there are certain principles that we should have learned from him.

1) Prayer involves waiting. Prayer is not just telling. Prayer is waiting. Prayer often means closing our lips so that our dear Lord might have his turn to speak. We need to allow him the opportunity to enter into our thought processes with his reply. It is a good thing to be silent at first, resting in the awareness that we are in the presence of the Lord. If we are willing to wait and be silent, we may find ourselves speaking out about things that we had never expected to mention. Such an approach also gives the Holy Spirit the

opportunity to intercede for us. Remember Romans 8:26? Let the Spirit speak on your behalf!

2) Prayer should not expect perfection of itself. It should not surprise us that we are not yet perfectly trusting children of God. Christ is not yet fully formed in us. We remain torn between doubt and trust. We are afraid to go ahead. Doubt seems to have won out. We become extremely critical of ourselves. We decide that all this is proof that we are guilty of terrible unbelief. But unbelief and doubt are not the same thing. Unbelief is the refusal to turn to God. Doubt is faith in distress, but nevertheless faith as it continues to tell God how troubled the heart is.

3) Prayer leads to the assurance that God is and always will be working for our good. We think again of Jesus saying, "Abba! Father! Your will be done." Most of us have learned many times over that it is often impossible to tell whether something is a blessing or a misfortune at the time it is happening. (Yes, this includes those who become million dollar lottery winners! Maybe them most of all.) In many respects, the real answer is in our hands, and ours alone, as we make use of a given moment as an opportunity to place ourselves into the hands of a heavenly Father. It is when we become willing to believe that he will lead us through whatever difficulties we are encountering, that we will experience true peace and rest.

Such confidence does not come easily, and it would be a great mistake to imagine the prayers of Jesus being free of those struggles that are a part of our condition, sinless though he was. We tend to pass over too quickly the picture of Jesus in prayer as it is given to us in the Scriptures. He was in every respect our brother, in every respect sharing our agonies, in every respect tempted as we are (Heb. 4:15); and it was through prayer to his "Abba, Father" as he faced a hostile crowd, or knelt in Gethsemane, or hung from the cross, that he was "made perfect" and "became the source of eternal salvation for all who obey him" (Heb. 5:9).

According to our needs and the circumstances of the day, may each of the prayers offered by Jesus help us to make a good beginning to our own prayers. May our prayers in communion with Jesus, our living Lord, lead us into the presence of the Father as we press on to the goal of becoming his obedient and trusting children.

SHOUTS, CRIES, AND PRAYERS: PSALMS FOR THE DAYS OF LENT

We have seen how the last days of Jesus were marked by petitions offered up with what the letter to the Hebrews aptly describes as "loud cries and tears" (Heb. 5:7). It is a phrase that calls to mind the great prayers in the book of Psalms, "the prayer book of the Bible." In fact, it was in the actions and words of Jesus that so many of the psalms find their ultimate meaning.

Consequently, the use of parallel psalms is an excellent way by which to reinforce or enter more deeply into the prayers of Jesus examined in this book. The psalms can become a stimulus for one's own prayers by using the following procedure: 1) read a psalm; 2) reflect upon it; 3) listen to God; 4) finally, speak to him. One might also keep a personal journal of prayers.

A pastor or an educational director may wish to reprint the reflections on the psalms that are here offered, or offer their own "customized" devotional thoughts for fellow members of the congregation. Psalms are presented for each day in the season of Lent, with each week centering on a theme related to Jesus' prayers as he drew ever closer to the cross.

Above all, it is important to remember that while prayer may take many forms, before anything else it is an attitude of the heart. It is entering into the presence of God. This is the greatest lesson we can learn from Jesus concerning prayer. He was in communion with the Father. This should be our primary aim in looking to Jesus as the model for the godly life.

Week 1: How Jesus began his task
Theme for the week: Communion with God

Day 1: Psalm 1

In memory of their father a family planted an oak seedling on the grounds of the church he loved so much. They planted it because he had been a man firmly rooted in the Word of the Lord. The tree is growing taller and sturdier each year. The soil is good and its roots are going deep. Let every soul become like that tree, reaching for the living waters of the Lord instead of becoming a drifting, windblown tumble-weed.

Day 2: Psalm 23

Too often this psalm, like the Lord's Prayer, has been reduced to nothing more than a cliché. In its greatness it deserves deep reflection, not mere repetition. How ought we give thanks for the still waters and green pastures of the past and the present? If at this moment we are walking through one of life's deep ravines, are we ready to tell the Lord that we know that we do not walk alone? How can we possibly speak of the Lord's goodness and mercy without a prayer of thanks to him who said, "I am the good shepherd. The good shepherd lays down his life for the sheep"?

Day 3: Psalm 3

There are people who think that faith in God is of no help at all. They don't just think it. They say it. But try telling that to Jesus. The record is clear. He was in constant communion with the Father; and while this did not mean that his enemies vanished into thin air, through prayer he found the strength to withstand them all. If you are troubled at this moment, speak the words of hope in this psalm as words from your own heart. They will be heard by your Father. They will bring new life to your spirit.

Day 4: Psalm 147:1-11

The writers of the psalms were never afraid to ask, "Why?" But if there are tears in the psalms, there also is holy laughter. There is the kind of joy that Jesus expressed as he saw prisoners set free, the sick healed, light breaking in where before there was only darkness, and the heavenly Father clothing the lilies of the field. Let us, with the saints on earth and the saints above and all the company of heaven, lift up our voices in praise of the Lord.

Day 5: Psalm 127

We all are in the construction business. We are engaged in building the home, the church, and our own personal lives. In each case our labor would be in vain except for the Lord's help. A house is made complete when it is a home built on a foundation of love and esteem. Members of the church receive the call, "Like living stones be yourselves built into a spiritual house" (1 Peter 2:5). Each one of us has a body that is "a temple of the Holy Spirit within you" (1 Cor. 6:19). O Lord, help us to build aright. Without you, our labor will be in vain.

Day 6: Psalm 131

There are so many conflicting demands and difficult choices. What should I pray? What can I say? I need to remember that prayer is more than my talking all the time. Communing with God also is listening. It is listening without fidgeting. When speaking of the presence of God, the psalms call on us to remember the touch of our father's hand and the warmth of our mother's breast. As a child snuggled safe in a parent's embrace knows so well, some of life's best answers come in times of quietness.

Day 7: Psalm 139

You don't have to be old to be lonely. You can be quite young and yet feel the same way. It happens when you feel like there is no one around who really cares what's going on inside of you. Everybody is too busy doing their own thing. But what about God? What an antidote to loneliness it is to remember, with the psalmist, that the Lord who is above me and below me, and infinitely beyond me, is also within me. Like the air we breathe, God is round about us in Christ, engulfing us in his all-sufficient grace.

Week 2: Jesus' prayer for our spiritual healing
Theme for the week: Renew a right spirit within me

Day 1: Psalm 25:1-7

Who can straighten us out? Who can bring us back? Who but the Lord? In the verses before us, a veritable avalanche of verbs pours from the psalmist's heart as he describes how the Lord can help us. Mark them one by one. It is the Lord who will save us from shame, enable us to know his ways, teach us, lead us, be mindful of his ways of mercy, and forgetful of our past. Can God really forget the sins of our youth? He can and he does! God forgives as completely as a program that has been cleared from a computer disk, gone forever, wiped clean.

Day 2: Psalm 25:8-15

Can we, with all our glaring faults and weaknesses, ask of the Lord all those blessings proclaimed in this psalm? Dare we turn to him for pardon, insight, prosperity, friendship, rescue, grace, companionship, relief, forgiveness, deliverance, refuge, and redemption? Yes, all this and more, for the expectations of the psalmist reach their fullness in the experience of Christ in our lives. By God's grace we may join in the apostle's exultation: "Praise be to the God and Father of our Lord Jesus Christ, who has bestowed on us in Christ every spiritual blessing. . . . In union with Christ Jesus he raised us up and enthroned us with him in the heavenly realms, so that he might display in the ages to come how immense are the resources of his grace" (Eph. 1:3; 2:6-7 NEB).

Day 3: Psalm 51:1-5

It is relatively easy to admit, in broad generalities, that we are sinners. It's something else to hold up before God specific sins and name them. But why must we do this? Doesn't God already know them? It is to be done for our sake, not his. It is after we name a sin that we can next surrender it and give it over to God. It is after such surrender that God can then begin the process of healing and cleansing, so that our joy may be restored.

Day 4: Psalm 51:6-14

The tabernacle of the Lord was not much to look at from the outside as it was carried through the wilderness. Its outer walls were made of the rough skin of animals. Ah, but the inside! There one would see fine linens, precious stones, and vessels of gold. The beauty was on the inside. Our body also is a temple. It is not our own, however; it is the Lord's. It is "the temple of the Holy Spirit within you" (1 Cor. 6:19). To what have we been giving the most attention, the exterior or the interior of that temple? The psalmist would have us pray with him, "Create a right spirit within me. . . . Take not thy Holy Spirit from me."

Day 5: Psalm 51:15-19

The church is like a hospital. It is a place of healing. So was the Temple of ancient times, and the rites and sacrifices God ordered for it were all aimed at helping his people to recognize their sin, rejoice in the mercy of God, and rededicate themselves to living for the Lord. But human nature has a great capability for taking something good and rendering it useless. The Lord does not want us to put on a show for him. He wants our hearts. What good does it do to go to a hospital if we will not take our medicine or allow the surgeon's knife to pierce our skin? It's always the right time to say, "My sacrifice, O God, is a broken spirit?" (51:17, NEB).

Day 6: Psalm 56:8-11

The disciple Peter wept bitterly after those around him had taken advantage of his fears and caused him to deny the Lord. Must not we do the same? But then what? With the psalmist, we can ask God to put our tears in a bottle! Among certain peoples of the Middle East the tears of mourners were kept in a bottle as a memorial to the departed one. The tears are ours. The bottle is God's. We can ask God to remember our weeping as the sacrifice of a broken spirit, which he always desires. And then, knowing that God is on our side, we can face those enemies again. We can leave the weeping of the night behind us and walk again in the light of his love.

Day 7: Psalm 50

Not everyone who goes to church goes to God. Remember the parable about the priest and Levite who hurried past the man who had fallen among thieves and lay half-dead along the side of the road? Perhaps they were hurrying to the Temple to offer their sacrifices. In this psalm, however, the Lord reminds us that he does not need the sacrifices of animals because his followers think he is hungry. Nor does he have any wounds to bind. It is his children who are hungry and hurting, physically and emotionally. If we are truly thankful for the healing he has brought to us, show it, he says, by our love for one another and by choosing the path of righteousness.

Week 3: "Abba, Father!"
Theme for the week: Letting go and letting God

Day 1: Psalm 46

The magnificent imagery of this psalm inspired Martin Luther to write "A Mighty Fortress Is Our God." In it we see God as the Lord of creation (vv. 1–3), history (vv. 4–7), and everlasting peace (vv. 8–11). It continues to inspire and mold faith. For 50 years,

Randolph Haugen was the editor of the annual, *Christmas.* His daughter, Mary, wrote about the effect of his daily reading of the Scripture upon her life and the life of her children, "I can hear my father reading 'God is my refuge and strength' right now. I use this psalm and Psalm 121 as the Bible passages I send in my letters to our children at college. They speak of God's majesty and power, but also his protection and his help. These words describe the Lord I know and love."

Day 2: Psalm 57

Sickness, reverses, duplicity, faithlessness, treachery, and disappointment may all come our way even though we have given ourselves to the Lord. The psalmist refuses to be intimidated. His faith defies them all: "My heart is steadfast, O God, my heart is steadfast. I will sing and make melody!" (v. 7). The apostle Paul showed that same grit when he said, "We are afflicted in every way, but not crushed; perplexed, but not driven to despair; persecuted, but not forsaken" (2 Cor. 4:8-9). God lives. Christ lives. And I shall live, too!

Day 3: Psalm 34

I dare you, the psalmist says, to try out the promises of God and see if he will not help you. Many have fretted away a lifetime because they could not learn to do this. If only we would listen to Jesus. Time after time, he has assured us that our heavenly Father listens, answers, and gives to us all that we could ever need (Luke 11:1-13, Matt. 6:25-34).

Day 4: Psalm 107:1-22, 33-43

The greater the need, the higher should be our words of praise and thanksgiving. This divine principle is taught by the apostle Paul when he writes,

"In everything by prayer and supplication with thanksgiving let your requests be made known to God" (Phil. 4:6). It is demonstrated in Psalm 107. He delivers us from the desert, from the prison, from illness, from sea storms, from drought. Are we "diminished and brought low through oppression, trouble and sorrow" (v. 39)? If we are wise, that is exactly the time to remember the steadfast love of the Lord (v. 43). Such remembrance will give us the strength and the peace we need.

Day 5: Psalm 107:23-32

How great the storms of life! How high the waves! We are like the sailors: "They mounted up to heaven, they went down to the depths" (v. 26). We must cling to the mast and wait for the Lord to calm the storm. Then, as the waves begin to subside, faith should take the next step. We should start looking for the tops of the mountains. This picture is suggested by the story of the great flood. While Noah's ark was still surrounded by the waters of the deep, we are told, they looked out and behold, "the tops of the mountains were seen" (Gen. 8:5). Seeing this, Noah took heart and began to send out testings. Instead of concentrating on the destruction around him, he looked ahead to those signs that would be a confirmation of God's gracious promise to save him. There is no reason why we should not do the same.

Day 6: Psalm 30

Those who wish to give thanks for a rescue they have experienced, as well as those who want to affirm their confidence that God will deal with them in the future as he has in the past, will find this psalm of great help. Within it is one of the richest sentences in all literature: "Weeping may tarry for the night, but joy comes in the morning." God is always more ready to give than we to ask. He is listening before we speak. Take heart, O my soul. He is shaping new joys for me even while I sleep. How foolish then, to give over my cares to the Lord at night, only to wake in the morning and take them upon my shoulders again, trudging heavily through the day as if I had never heard that his favor is for a lifetime.

Day 7: Psalm 43

Psalm 43 is the prayer of a person in exile, living out his lonely days among the Hebrews held captive in Babylonia. How he longed for the good old days back home, dreaming of going once more up the holy hill to Zion. There are exiles everywhere. There was the "prodigal son" who was in exile in a "far country" because he was alienated from his father. Then he heard a voice within him telling him to go home where he belonged. O my soul, go back to God. Ascend the sacred hill whereon the Son of God died for us all. Hope in God. He will never disappoint you.

Week 4: Father, glorify thy name
Theme for the week: Glorifying God

Day 1: Psalm 119:9-16

We all have heard much talk about committing ourselves to the Lord; but, as a good friend once reminded me, "We've all been called to present our bodies as living sacrifices to the Lord. The trouble is, we keep crawling off the altar." That's why Lutherans pray in their "Brief Order for Confession and Forgiveness," (*Lutheran Book of Worship*, p. 56), "Forgive us, renew us and lead us, so that we may *delight* in your will and walk in your ways, to the *glory* of your holy name." Through the word of pardon spoken in the name of Jesus Christ, we know we can crawl back on again, ready once more to say with the psalmist, "I will *delight* in thy statutes; I will not forget thy word" (v. 15).

Day 2: Psalm 141

As we envision our prayers rising up to the Lord as incense, the beauty of this imagery should not be allowed to obscure the powerful prayer that follows. It is a prayer in which the lines of battle are clearly drawn. The writers of the psalms were good at that. They were not afraid to state clearly what we prefer to deny, soften, or avoid: The forces of evil are running wild in this world, seeking to destroy what is good.

The psalm also raises questions about how much our lives are glorifying the name of God. Am I forever blurting out something I then wish I could take back? What kind of company do I keep? What kind of deals are being offered me that I find hard to reject? Have I begun to act as if I am the one person in the world who can do as I please without stepping on a booby trap?

Day 3: Psalm 19

The glory of the whole creation calls us to recognize the power and majesty of the Lord. This same Lord speaks to us through his Word, which we can count on all the way as the source of spiritual strength and growth. *"The law of the Lord is perfect, reviving the soul"* (v. 7). It leads us to say: "I want to grow. I want to be cleansed of 'hidden' faults, that is, faults still hidden from my own self-awareness. Yes, my willingness to commit myself to the Lord includes the risk of self-confrontation and the change that will then be asked of me, not by others, but by my own conscience. It's scary to say this, Lord, but I want to be changed."

Day 4: Psalm 24

This psalm often is called a messianic psalm. It points to the coming of the Lord's "anointed one," the "Messiah" (Hebrew) or the "Christ" (Greek). Most certainly we can see in it a picture of Jesus as the Christ, one completely committed to serving his heavenly Father, and himself the mighty King of glory whom we welcome into our hearts.

The psalm not only speaks about Christ. It also speaks about Christ in us. For Christ has come and through his promised Spirit now lives in us. He lives in us in order to make us able to pray and to do the things he first did. O Father, I praise you for the holiness of your only Son, and I ask for his power to lead me more deeply into a life that will glorify your name.

Day 5: Psalm 91

This psalm makes its point so clearly, Lord. If we put ourselves totally into your hands, nestling beneath your protecting wings, we will find shelter from all our enemies. It's there for all to read: The Lord will deliver us when we commit ourselves to his ways.

What a surprise, then, that verses 10 and 11 are the very words the devil used to tempt Jesus, suggesting that he could gain an army of instant followers if only he would cast himself down from the pinnacle of the temple and then walk away unscathed. Wouldn't it be great for Jesus to present himself as the star of the "Aerial Show of the Ages, Proof Positive of the Power of God!" That's not how Jesus saw it.

Whenever we begin to think of the great impression we will make on others through our demonstration of faith and God's consequent care for us, we are headed for trouble. No, let us put ourselves into his care with only one prayer: that *his* name be glorified, not ours.

Day 6: Psalm 111

Most of us are long on requests but short on thanksgiving. Even the prayers in church seem to be set up that way. And yet I know that some of my deepest experiences of Christian fellowship have come when I have been joined to a friend in Christ in giving heartfelt thanks and praise for the things God has done for us. O Lord, not only in the privacy of my room, but also in the presence of others I will praise you. "I will give thanks to the Lord with my whole heart, in the company of the upright, in the congregation" (v. 1).

Day 7: Psalm 33

A woodpecker had just begun to hammer away at a tree when a bolt of lightning struck that tree and sent it crashing to the ground. The woodpecker could not help but congratulate himself on the power he was developing in his blows. Foolish woodpecker! Foolish humankind! When will we learn to give glory to God as we remember that "A king is not saved by his great army; a warrior is not delivered by his great strength. The war horse is a vain hope for victory, and by its great might it cannot save" (vv. 16, 17)?

Week 5: His prayer for forgiveness
Theme for the week: Forgiveness

Day 1: Psalm 32

When we remember that *blessed* means "happy," the opening words of this psalm, "*Happy* is he whose transgression is forgiven," leap out at us with new meaning. With one broad stroke the psalmist destroys the myth of the happy sinner. It is a grave misconception that the people of God go around morose and miserable while others are singing and dancing their way through life. This psalm reminds us that the breakthrough to joy comes to those who seek forgiveness from the Lord. "Many are the pangs of the wicked; but steadfast love surrounds those who trust in the Lord" (v. 10).

Day 2: Psalm 103

If I had kept count, I wouldn't be surprised to find that in my role as pastor I have shared this psalm with more parishioners than any other. I have used it so frequently because it touches on so many of the blessings God brings to us. We are dust, we are grass, we are weak and frail children. But our heavenly Father remembers us, renews us, forgives us. He restores our strength both physically and spiritually.

In biblical usage, to "bless" the Lord means to speak well of and praise the Lord for his activity in our lives. No matter what our condition might be, the psalm calls on us to search out our many reasons for saying, "Bless the Lord, O my soul!" Especially, O my soul, for the presence of Jesus Christ in my life. Without him at my side, I would soon go down into the dust.

Day 3: Psalm 25

In the Hebrew this is an acrostic psalm, meaning that each consecutive verse begins with the next letter from the Hebrew alphabet. Like a skilled, careful craftsman the psalmist leads us into the help we can surely find in God.

Make your plea known to God, he says (vv. 1–3). Remind yourself of the merciful ways in which God has "from of old" dealt with his people. Count on him to deal with you in exactly the same way (vv. 4–7). As we read the words of this psalm concerning the "ways of God," let us pray for the vision to see Jesus standing behind them. We can fix our hope on the free forgiveness offered for "thy name's sake, O Lord" (v. 11).

Day 4: Psalm 130

The two kids were dropped off along the highway and began to walk down a long, stony road to a cottage where their parents waited for them. It was very late, clouds blotted out the stars above, and there was not a light along the way. They learned what "pitch black" really means as they literally inched their way along. They could not help but wonder if it would not be best simply to sit down and wait for the morning.

Eventually, each of us learns what it means to call out from depths so deep that no light from above can be seen. In the soul's dark night, we are like those who wait for the morning. Then the light of God's steadfast love dawns. We learn that the most awesome thing about God is his forgiveness and acceptance of sinners. We are lifted up on our feet again, and a light shines upon our path as we whisper, "My hope is built on nothing less than Jesus' blood and righteousness."

Day 5: Psalm 84

Why do some people have such a deep longing to be found "in the courts of the Lord"? Why is going to church such a big thing? Dietrich Bonhoeffer writes, "The present and gracious God, who is in Christ who in turn is in his congregation, is the fulfillment of all thanksgiving, all joy, and all longing in the psalms. As Jesus, in whom God himself dwells, longed for fellowship with God because he had become a man as we (Luke 2:49), so he prays with us for the total nearness and presence of God with those who are his" (*Psalms, the Prayer Book of the Bible* [Minneapolis: Augsburg, 1974], p. 41). It is the discovery of the presence of him who is our Redeemer that makes one day in his courts better than a thousand elsewhere.

Day 6: Psalm 55:1-23

This psalm is a prophecy concerning the suffering of Christ. We see the suffering servant of God going down and down, right to the bottom of the pit. Abandonment and treachery are the weapons used against him. No day was ever darker than the day of the death of the Son of God. Never was God more despised and rejected by humanity. But never was more accomplished by God! It is from the depths that the highest heights are scaled. Christ is lifted up for all the world to see, and the good news is proclaimed: "Your iniquity is pardoned!" O my soul, receive this good news and climb up with him to new heights of joy!

Day 7: Psalm 4

The Revised Standard Version alternates in its translation of the Hebrew between "Have mercy on me" and "Be gracious to me." Psalm 4:1 and Psalm 51:1 are asking for the same thing, the gift we all need the most: the mercy of God. Jesus tells us that the tax collector prayed, "God, be merciful to me a sinner" (Luke 18:13). The blind men along the Jericho road cried out, "Lord, have mercy on us, Son of David" (Matt. 20:31). The direct prayer that God would "be gracious" or "have mercy" is found 20 times in the Psalter. There will never be a time when human beings will not need to speak this prayer, and never a time when we are not extended the invitation, "Let us then with confidence draw near to the throne of grace, that we may receive mercy and find grace to help in the time of need" (Heb. 4:16).

Week 6: Why hast thou forsaken me?
Theme for the week: Courage

Day 1: Psalm 22:1-21

This psalm portrays the dereliction of Christ on the cross in a most remarkable way. Read verses 1–18 (noting especially verses 8 and 18) and let your mind leap 1000 years ahead to see the anguish of the psalmist fulfilled in Christ. (Hebrews 2:12 also places v. 22 in the mouth of Christ.) Dietrich Bonhoeffer writes, "David himself may have once prayed this psalm in his own song. If so, he did this as king, anointed by God and, therefore, persecuted by men, from whom Jesus Christ would descend. He did it as the one who bore Christ in himself. But Christ himself used this prayer and for the first time gave it its full meaning" (*Psalms: The Prayer Book of the Bible*, p. 36). The taste of death in his mouth, his body pierced by nails, his clothes divided among his executioners, he still cries out to God. Behold the man, O my soul. He was abandoned for me!

Day 2: Psalm 13

Because this week's meditation reflects on the cry of Jesus found also in Psalm 22, it is easy to focus on negative terms such as dereliction and abandonment. But the writers of the psalms, so ready to admit their deepest feelings of despair, also show the result of pouring out one's heart to God. The courage to hold onto God is renewed. The psalmist here speaks of his plight, then asks for help, and commits himself to the promise of deliverance. Prayer to God does not lead us to give up. It makes us able to hold on.

Day 3: Psalm 10

Today's psalm boldly compares the wicked to robbers and fierce beasts of the forest. They act as if they can get away with anything, and sometimes it seems that they do! But then the psalmist shows what happens when we pour out before God the questions that trouble us. Faith revives. But before there can be faith, there must be questions and doubts. Before there can be courage, there must be fear. While we, like our Savior upon the cross, wait in this world of darkness, faith says, "Lord, you will set all things right. I just know you will. Even so, Lord, come quickly!"

Day 4: Psalm 42

Few of us live where we will see wild animals coming to a brook to quench their thirst. I don't. But one winter morning I saw a blue jay vainly trying to slake its thirst at the frozen bird bath in front of my kitchen window. He kept pecking away, but it did no good.

The psalmist is like that blue jay. He desires that God would be for him a fountain of living water. To that point the thirst remains, but he still hangs on. So should we. What seems to be a time of spiritual dryness can really be a sign that we are experiencing growing pains. Maybe 10 years ago we thought we had everything in our spiritual life just where we wanted it. If now we feel a thirst for God we did not know then, this may well be a sign of growth. Now we are drawing closer to Jesus who stands by the well and says, "Whoever drinks of the water that I shall give him will never thirst" (John 4:14).

Day 5: Psalm 31

The psalmist not only tells of his own agonies, he also foretells the suffering and agony that will befall the Christ. Thinking of such desperate circumstances, we might fail to notice that the final word, "Be strong, and let your heart take courage" (v. 24), bears witness to Christ's courage. Courage, let us always remember, is not the *absence* of fear. Courage is the *companion* of fear. An American hero of another generation, Captain Eddie Rickenbacker, once said, "Courage is doing what you're afraid to do. There can be no courage unless you're scared." O Lord Jesus, model for our prayers, help us to live with your kind of courage as we face those things that cause us to fear!

Day 6: Psalm 143

The person who wrote this psalm was in deep trouble. As we read it, we think of how Jesus must have felt and prayed as his own days drew to an end and he faced the cup held out before him. "Although he was a Son, he learned obedience through what he suffered" (Heb. 5:8). We must look at life and our time in prayer from this standpoint, too. We don't have a push-button God. We have a God who will help us to grow, through prayer, into an ever deeper relationship with him. The psalmists kept praying, and they kept growing. The same possibility is open to us.

Day 7: Psalm 22:22-31

Psalm 22 points to the dereliction of Christ as he hung upon the cross, but we dare not overlook how it also expresses a spirit of hope, which we should emulate. The psalmist has faith that he will go from abandonment to fulfillment, from dereliction to victory. "This is the victory that overcomes the world, our faith" (1 John 5:4). The closing verses of this psalm describe the full and complete victory which will be gained by the perfectly obedient Christ, the Son of God. In him we find hope for our final victory. "O death, where is thy victory? O death, where is thy sting? . . . Thanks be to God, who gives us the victory through our Lord Jesus Christ" (1 Cor. 15:55, 57).

Week 7: *He shows me how to die*
Theme for the week: *The victorious Christ*

Holy Wednesday: Psalm 88

As the days of Holy Week move on, we are drawn ever closer to the mystery of the passion of Christ. Perhaps the psalmist is expressing a sorrow that goes beyond one's own experience. Perhaps not. But who can claim to have matched the sorrows of Christ, the Savior of the world? Better to say of this psalm, "In it I see the sorrows he endured for me, that I might be free."

Maundy Thursday: Psalm 114

This psalm is known as a Passover psalm, recalling, as it does, the rescue of the people of God from their slavery in Egypt. On this day we remember how Christ used the Passover to give us a new meal in which we are assured that as far as the east is from the west, so far has he removed our transgressions from us. This is a night for remembering that, while it is the individual who must have faith, faith is never individualistic. A believing child of God always seeks community with the rest of God's children. On this night, that means coming together for a time of quiet confession, pardon, and the nourishment of the body and blood of the Lord in his holy supper.

Good Friday: Psalm 2

The time for the setting of the sun is not far away. Already a quietness lies over the battlefield. The battle against God has been fought. The slain one has been removed from the field and taken to his final resting place. But who has won? Even now, in the bowels of the earth, God is stirring and preparing to give the nations to his Son. Already we can look beyond death and toward new life!

Holy Saturday: Psalm 98

It would be difficult to find a psalm that more eloquently describes Christ's transition from a state of suffering to one of triumph. It is a psalm to be said aloud with great joy, from beginning to end, for after all his suffering, Christ has at last gained the victory.

O my soul, you have dwelt much on the suffering of your Lord. Learn now from him "who for the joy that was set before him, endured the cross, despising the shame, and is seated at the right hand of the throne of God" (Heb. 12:2). It is when we think that we stand secure that we fall. It is when we are un-armed except for our faith, helpless in the sight of the world, that we shall be saved.

Easter: Psalm 118

Songs of victory fill the vaults of heaven as we hear the angels and all the saints of old sing out, "Welcome, risen Lord Jesus! Welcome, King of glory, our Lord strong and mighty, our Lord mighty in battle! The gates of the everlasting city are opened to you that you might come in. Come, sit at the right hand of the throne of God, O King, for you have been tested, but have prevailed. You have gained the name which is above every name and before you we kneel in unending praise."